Teaching Young Adults

Technological and employment change in Europe is intense. Preparing young adults for this environment requires that fundamental changes are made to the present education system. Motivating and retaining young people is difficult; many leave education with little to show for the years spent, and little to offer employers. This book is a much needed handbook for teachers, managers and policy makers; it provides insights and practical strategies to make education more relevant to the lives and needs of young adults.

Teaching Young Adults offers practical solutions based on original research – carried out across Europe – into the communication styles of teachers and learners, and into the constructs that students use when informally evaluating their teachers. The authors suggest that the current provision of education is out of touch with the needs of many young adults in the growing post-compulsory sector; but they argue that even within the present flawed system, teachers should work with young adults in ways which form the foundation of lifelong learning. This book will be an invaluable, up-to-date handbook for teachers on PGCE training for secondary, further and higher education; students of education at undergraduate and postgraduate level; education managers and policy makers.

Joe Harkin is Reader in Education at Oxford Brookes University, and was lead consultant nationally in the development of key skills in communication. **Gill Turner** is currently working at Oxford Brookes University with Joe Harkin on the Communication Styles of Teachers project and completing her PhD. **Trevor Dawn** is a lecturer in Education at Oxford Brookes University and trains teachers who work in Secondary, Further and Adult Education in Active Learning Strategies.

Teaching Young Adults

A handbook for teachers in
post-compulsory education

Joe Harkin, Gill Turner
and Trevor Dawn

London and New York

First published 2001 by RoutledgeFalmer
11 New Fetter Lane, London EC4P 4EE

Simultaneously published in the USA and Canada
by RoutledgeFalmer
29 West 35th Street, New York, NY 10001

RoutledgeFalmer is an imprint of the Taylor & Francis Group

Typeset in Baskerville by
BOOK NOW Ltd
Printed and bound in Great Britain by
TJ International, Padstow, Cornwall

British Library Cataloguing in Publication Data
A catalogue record for this book is available from the British Library

Library of Congress Cataloging-in-Publication Data
Harkin, Joe, 1946–
    Teaching young adults : a handbook for teachers in further education / Joe Harkin, Gill
Turner, and Trevor Dawn.
        p.   cm.
    Includes bibliographical references and index.
    1. High school teaching–Great Britain. 2. College teaching–Great Britain. 3.
Continuing Education–Great Britain–4. Learning. I. Turner, Gill, 1960–II. Dawn,
Trevor, 1941–III. Title.

LB1607.53.G7 H37 2000
373.1102 – dc21   00–042479

ISBN 0-415-22284-2
ISBN 0-415-22283-4 (Hbk)

Contents

List of figures

List of tables

Acknowledgements

Thanks are extended to many teachers on in-service training courses who have contributed ideas and tried out ideas in order to engage young adults more actively in learning. Thanks also to the teachers and their students who have taken part in the communication styles research; and to the students who contributed their views about effective teaching to the Quali-teach project.

Introduction

This book combines three topics: theories of learning; practical strategies to engage learners; and self-directed professional development. It is intended to help teacher trainers and teachers to link professional development with learner development in ways that may foster a community of adults of all ages learning together.

Both the theory of learning and strategies for teaching have been dealt with more fully in other texts, but it is in the bringing together of the three topics that this book breaks new ground. In doing so, it aims to connect issues of general policy, learning theory, and the practice of learning and teaching in ways that will help teachers to work more effectively with young adult learners.

'Young adult' is taken loosely to refer to the age group 14–25, in schools, colleges and universities. The case studies and research that inform Parts II and III of the book are based on work in all three settings, and with teachers and learners on programmes from basic skills, where some learners had emotional and behavioural difficulties; through GCSE, A level and GNVQ, to undergraduate and some postgraduate study.

The book is the fruit of several endeavours: work with teachers in training, especially on in-service City and Guilds 730 and Certificate in Education programmes; research into the communication styles of teachers and learners; and research into student views of post-16 education as part of a European funded, Socrates project.

The structure of the book

The book is divided into three parts and a conclusion. Part I is an overview of the context in which teachers and young adults work together at learning. It deals with three broad issues: student disaffection from education, the profound technological change that affects all teachers and learners, and the response to these factors by government policy. Chapter 2 extends this analysis to three particularly important topics that affect learning: the growth of telematics, new insights into human learning, and the introduction of key skills.

Part II examines three interlocking areas of theory: theories of *learning*, theories of the role of *learners*, and theories of the role of *teachers*.

Part III exemplifies the *practice* of learning and teaching. Chapter 6 gives examples of learning theories in practice and shows teachers how they may engage learners more actively in the process of learning. Chapter 7 gives examples of teachers who have attempted to develop their practice in self-directed ways. Chapter 8 gives an account of the Communication Styles Questionnaire (CSQ) that teachers may use *with* their students to develop their patterns of working together.

Chapter 9 is intended to be a thought-provoking conclusion to the book that may be used as a basis for discussion of important issues in the education of young adults. It is an attempt to open a debate about the philosophy of working with young adults.

The book does not have to be read from cover to cover. Sections and even chapters may be read individually in order, for example, to review learning theories, or to develop strategies for more active learner involvement, or as a preparation for use of the Communication Styles Questionnaire.

Teachers will bring their own ideas and experience to the book and will build on the knowledge and examples given here. The end result is intended to be more active classrooms, in which young adult learners play a more engaged part in their own education than many do at the time of writing.

Part I

Major issues in the education of young adults

1 Responding to social and technological change

In future, the most successful nations will be those which develop high quality, skilled and motivated workforces and those which make the most of the talents of all their people.

The [UK] National Advisory Council for Education and Training Targets, 1994

Education and disaffection

Is all right with the state of education in Britain at the beginning of the twenty-first century? What do you think?

A colloquium organised by the Campaign for Learning and sponsored by the DfEE (Maxted, 1996) asked the question, 'But do the schools and, later, the colleges, universities and workplaces offer the best environment for learning and the best chance of engaging the learner?' The answer 'was a definite "no"'.

Too many learners, especially it was thought in secondary education, are unengaged and fail to achieve their potential. Too many young people leave compulsory schooling with little to show for the years spent. 'Certainly, in further and higher education there is still, it seems, too much pedagogy, too much *tabula rasa* "teaching". . .'. The continuing education of adults fares no better, with far too many closed off from education and training that builds on their experience in employment and private life.

> A child begins his or her life eager and curious to know the world, reaching out and touching what is not understood. Sometimes it comes apart in their hands. The light (this light of curiosity) goes out as they make the inexorable march into the formal education system.
>
> Crequer, 1996

Delegates from European countries and the United States at a symposium in 1996 on *The Future of Training and Vocational Education in the Global Economy* (Harkin, 1997), regardless of the structure of their country's education and training system, maintained that traditional pedagogy is blocking curriculum reform of education and training. Government policies have paid only scant attention to pedagogy and yet the low skills equilibrium of both the USA and the UK may be ascribed in part to the dominant cognitive orientation towards narrow special-isation and didacticism. Useful knowledge, as we shall see in Chapter 3, is constructed by learners in an interactive engagement with issues that matter to them; by contrast, much education and training post-14 is an agony of irrelevance and boredom that the bright and well motivated endure, while others drop out or fail. If governments are serious about improving the skills and motivation of the workforce, then they must take pedagogy seriously.

In the closing years of the twentieth century, there was what amounted to a crusade by successive governments to raise the level of retention and achieve-ment of young people. The main weapons in this crusade were benchmarking, inspections, and funding arrangements to reward successful institutions. Despite this flurry of exhortation to increase retention and achievement, the figures for both showed only slow improvement, leading to the White Paper, *Learning to Succeed* (DfEE, 1999a) declaring that 'Aspirations and staying on rates remain too low. The system fails a significant section of the community, often the most vulnerable.' Statistical evidence to the Kennedy Report (FEFC, 1997a) showed that at 16 over 80 per cent of people were receiving some form of education; by age 17 this had dropped to about 75 per cent; and by 18 to less than 60 per cent. The drop-out was disproportionately among young people from lower social classes, and some ethnic minorities. The Minister for Lifelong Learning made it clear (Wicks,1999) that *Learning to Succeed* 'is absolutely central to what the government's about – it's about economics, but also about social policy'.

As ever, young people from relatively affluent backgrounds were doing well, staying on in school or college, achieving better results than their parents had, going on to a fast expanding university sector. Meanwhile, many other people were not succeeding in education. The Kennedy report held that 'Learning is a weapon against poverty and the route to participation and active citizenship.' (FEFC, 1997b) It is like the parable of the lost sheep in which the shepherd is less concerned for the ninety-nine sheep who are safe than for the one who is lost. There was more than one lost sheep at a time when government policy in *Learning to Succeed* (1999) declared that, 'The notion of "leaving education at sixteen" must pass into history'.

How do you find the lost sheep? The shepherd listens for its voice and in further education a number of studies in the late 1990s began to listen to the voice of learners, including those who had left early. Bloomer and Hodkinson (1999), by closely following the paths of some learners, showed how easy it is to be put on an inappropriate course; to be given the wrong advice; to be inadequately supported in the education process. Whereas some learners, possibly supported by knowledgeable parents or peers, know what they want and how to achieve it, more vulnerable and isolated people may need closer personal support.

A survey of 9,000 students, including those who had withdrawn from courses (Martinez and Munday, 1998), found a general satisfaction with the quality of teaching but a marked dissatisfaction among students who had withdrawn. The dissatisfaction was particularly directed at *teachers* as distinct from *teaching*. The relationship with teachers is a crucially important factor in both student satis-faction and student dissatisfaction (Harkin and Turner, 1997; Johannessen *et al.*, 1997; Harkin, 1998) showing how vital to the learning experience is the role and behaviour of the teacher and interaction between teachers and learners.

Education and technological change

Education and training do not, of course, exist in a vacuum. They are part of a wider social fabric of values, families, employment and civic life. What happens within education is, in part, dependent on what happens outside education, in homes, communities and workplaces. It is wise to first step back from what happens between learners and teachers, in order to put teaching into its social context.

There is no deterministic relationship between technology, labour markets and education and training. Investment in education and training will not automatically produce higher levels of economic performance and other factors, such as capital investment, strategic economic planning and the buoyancy of the world economy, may all be more important. Besides which, the quality of human life is not measurable by economic indicators alone. Nevertheless, the knowledge explosion brought about by changes in technology is having a profound impact on the labour market and the ability of firms and countries to respond to these technological and labour market changes depends, in large measure, upon suitable corresponding changes in education and training provision. Technology has changed rapidly; there has been a 90 per cent loss of technology in the EU in the past 30 years, with profound consequences for the types of knowledge and skills needed in employment, and for patterns of employment. In the UK only 2 per cent of the workforce is employed in agriculture; 19 per cent, and declining, in manufacturing, and the rest in service industries of one sort or another. There has been little corresponding change in education and training provision; Drucker pointed out as long ago as 1969 that whereas there have been agricultural and industrial revolutions, there has been no corresponding change in education and training. Since 1969, technological change has intensified but education and training continue in modes more suited to mass production models of manu-facturing and master/servant models of labour relations. This is not to argue that there have not been pockets of change but these tend to be isolated and sometimes short-lived.

There are other systematic problems: for example, the tendency for highly trained and well paid people to receive a disproportionately high amount of further training, compared to low skilled and low paid workers. Eighty per cent of the unemployed in the EU are unskilled, without qualifications. Small and medium sized enterprises (SMEs) find it particularly hard to offer systematic training and most people are employed by SMEs. SMEs need to operate in clusters if they are to meet their training needs (and other needs, such as technology diffusion and export marketing), however, Finegold (1993: 70) quoting Porter, found that the mechanisms to facilitate clusters are weakest in the

USA and the UK. In the USA, it is recommended that firms should invest 5–7 per cent of payroll in training if their staff are to maintain the levels of knowledge and skill needed to remain competitive globally; yet even more modest targets of around 2 per cent are rejected as unaffordable by most firms. There are similar patterns of low levels of investment in training throughout the EU.

Most firms rely on the state to provide training, partly because they fear free loading competitors who do not train but poach; partly because training is rarely seen as a solution to problems of productivity and competitiveness; partly because it is assumed that the state should provide. State provision is mainly through tertiary institutions, such as colleges of further education (CFEs) in the UK and Community colleges in the USA. Typically, these institutions are poorly funded, have inadequate and out of date learning resources and, in keeping with other SMEs, are unable to train their own staff adequately to cope with change.

In response to continuous technological change, the optimal model of the organization, whether school, college or private enterprise, is the 'learning organisation', a community of practice characterised by features such as shared understandings of the nature of the enterprise by all staff; autonomous team working practices; problem solving; and open patterns of communication. Sadly, a reading of *North and South* (1854) by Mrs Gaskell, published in the early years of mass manufacturing shows that many of the divisions between management and labour portrayed there still exist: there are those who work with their 'heads' and others who are merely 'hands'. Here, a relatively humane mill owner is speaking:

> I maintain that despotism is the best kind of government for [workers]; so that . . . I must necessarily be an autocrat.

In retort to this, the central protagonist responds that

> . . . we must be mutually dependent. We may ignore our own dependence, or refuse to acknowledge that others depend on us in more respects than the payment of weekly wages; but the thing must be nevertheless.

The knowledge and skills that are central to this new, more communitarian working culture are the *key, core, work process, work shaping* skills or even *redundant* skills of the present system of education and training. Skills such as communicating effectively (orally and in writing; listening as well as speaking); working collaboratively with others; problem solving; taking responsibility for your own learning and work performance. In the UK, they are the skills acknowledged in the Confederation of British Industry document, *Towards a Skills Revolution* (1989) and the parallel Trades Union Congress document *Skills 2000* (1989). Unlike many, rapidly outdated, vocational skills, these key skills cannot be developed through didactic pedagogy, in which learners are relatively passive while teachers do most of the talking. These are *process* skills that can only be developed through a *process* in which individuals practise the skills in their everyday learning and work.

The advantages of people learning in situations in which they feel comfortable and in which they have a personal interest have long been known. For example, an OECD report of 1978 stated that:

> a large number [of Secondary pupils] in all countries lack motivation in school and later fail or under-achieve badly...What is now required is a radical re-thinking of this phase of education, taking the adolescent pupils and their views as the point of departure. This will involve widespread changes in curriculum, in personal relations, in assessment, and in guidance and orientation.

Psacharoupoulos and Woodhall, for the World Bank (1985) reported that, when the effects of school characteristics and family backgrounds were taken into account, students following specialist vocational tracks 'always scored significantly higher in both vocational and academic subjects'. Thus, the higher motivational effects of vocational study enabled students to succeed more, even in academic subjects, so that it is possible to have broad and balanced curricula based in a vocational context. This chimes with more recent research (Weston *et al.*, 1996) that showed significant gains to student learning as a result of work placements, especially for lower achievers.

In consequence of the materialism of our age, employment is a most important motivation for adult learners, young and old. The gaining of credentials that give access to secure, pleasant and well-paid employment is the motive for most learning beyond the early teens. This may be lamented by some who would prefer education to be devoted to what Matthew Arnold, the great Victorian poet and educator, referred to as the best that has been thought and said in the world – the great ideas and values and art of the past, handed on from generation to generation like a precious living flame that, if extinguished, will plunge us all into darkness. For some lucky people education is about Culture with a capital C, and Germans still use the term *bildung* to indicate that education and training are about this personal and cultural development, as well as the formation of skills and understanding. For most people in Britain, however, gaining a GCSE or NVQ or MBA is primarily about getting a decent job.

Not everyone, of course, will end up with a 'decent' job – secure, pleasant, well-paid. Hannah Arendt (1958) pointed out that in every European language, ancient and modern, there are two etymologically unrelated words for what we have come to think of as the same activity: *work* and *labour*. Work involves a period of dedicated training to learn a craft, a finished product or service in which to take pride, and respect from others for your craft knowledge. Labour involves using your body, the sweat of your brow, to sustain the means of life. If you drop dead someone else will do as well. The Russian verb for labour translates into our word *robot*.

Is most modern employment work or labour? Or have we developed a new form of employment that we call a *job*, neither work nor labour but bearing some characteristics of both? The traditional apprenticeship, leading to skilled work, has largely disappeared; much factory and other forms of labour has been replaced by robotic machines. Everyone involved in education post-14 should ponder the nature and needs of contemporary employment. If employment is the main motivator of education for this age group, then in large measure the process of schooling should offer an adequate preparation. Unfortunately, it has been recognised for a long time that this is not the case. As far back as 1921, the Newbolt Report claimed that education for most young people offered neither a broad-based, liberal experience of the sort that Matthew Arnold would have approved; nor an adequate preparation for employment. It was an impoverished affair that bored the pants off most learners. Have we advanced much since then?

If young people do not comprehend the nature of the learning journey that they are taking, and see no relationship between future employment and present education, it is likely that many will feel disorientated and downhearted. If there is high local unemployment, these feelings will be deepened. Paradoxically, the difficulty of gaining a 'decent' job decreases, rather than increases the motivation of many to gain credentials. The process is sometimes referred to as 'down-shifting', in which the fear of failure, and a belief that the effort is simply not worthwhile, leads people to withdraw their energies. The energy may still be there but shifted into other activities, positive or negative, music or sport; petty crime or drugs.

The concept of 'lifelong learning' refers simultaneously to the fact that current employment is in a state of almost permanent disequilibrium, in which technology, working practices, structures and roles are in constant flux; and to the expectation that the whole of the education system, not just that part that bears most directly on employment, will respond appropriately. An appropriate response may, however, require a paradigm shift, rather than piecemeal, small-scale change. The school leaving age has been raised several times; qualifications have been re-structured but, fundamentally, the formal education on offer today is little different to that offered at any time in the last century. Teachers may be exhorted and bullied into forcing learners *within the present system* to perform better but this may, at great emotional cost, only reinforce the inadequacies of the present model of education and training. Bored learners, disengaged at any deep, personal level from the process of education, may perform better, just as circus animals could be bullied into more wondrous tricks, but they will still remain bored and disengaged.

The Reform of British Education (or the practice of vulgar pragmatism)

Instead of fundamental change to the education system, in response to profound technological and social change, the tendency of succesive British governments, in keeping with similar tendencies in other countries, has been to attempt to modify existing structures, keeping in place the 'royal road' to high status qualifications, through A levels, and introducing piecemeal reforms in an effort to raise retention and achievement. This process was dubbed 'vulgar pragmatism' by Grubb (1999).

In Britain, the relationship between government and education changed fundamentally in 1976 when the then Prime Minister, James Callaghan, declared that British education was not equipping learners with the skills needed by industry. As the major investor in education, he maintained that government had a legitimate right to join with others to discuss and reform education. Since then, a series of reports have demanded more and better training, and successive governments have intervened in all phases of education, from nursery to university. The fundamental link made by Callaghan, between levels of education and economic performance, has been reinforced and all major political parties subscribe to what has become an orthodoxy of belief.

In secondary education, the policies of successive governments have increased selection and, therefore, specialisation (Chitty, 1992) in a way that may not bring about the radical transformations called for by the OECD report of 1978 quoted on page 7, but instead a regression to late nineteenth-century differentiation of educational opportunity, appropriate to one's 'station in life'. Such a regression is not only inimicable to social justice and out of keeping with the social cohesiveness needed in a democratic Europe, but also runs counter to the need to develop each individual to the full to achieve the UK targets for education and training; targets which already lag behind the current achievements of some other OECD countries.

The major government-led initiative to raise levels of participation in vocational education and training was the creation in 1986 of the National Council for Vocational Qualifications (NCVQ), charged with the task of turning what was widely regarded as a qualifications 'jungle' into a coherent and comprehensive framework of qualifications to be assessed to national standards. Two new qualifications were developed at great speed: National Vocational Qualifications (NVQs), which were intended to be employer-led; and General National Vocational Qualifications (GNVQs), or vocational A levels, designed to be broader-base qualifications, leading to either employment or higher education, and delivered by schools or colleges.

Employers – who it was intended should take primary responsibility for the delivery of NVQs – showed a marked reluctance to do so. While the national rhetoric of employers' organisations, such as the CBI, has been enthusiastic, the reality, especially among SMEs was a reluctance to train, and a reluctance to train in ways that are broader than job-specifics. Successive governments have been most unwilling to coerce employers to take training more seriously by, for example, a levy on turnover or profits. It is believed that this would reduce competitiveness and, in any case, that firms would find ways to circumvent the legislation. As a result, the intention that NVQs should be relatively broad-based qualifications, leading to the ability to transfer to new jobs, new employers and to higher education, has largely not been met.

The government targets for education, training and lifelong learning that, for example, by the end of the twentieth century 80 per cent of young people should be trained to NVQ level 2 or equivalent (GNVQ Intermediate; GCSE grade C in 4 subjects) and 50 per cent trained to NVQ level 3 or equivalent (GNVQ

Advanced; GCE A level in 2 subjects) were not achieved. The participation of young people beyond compulsory schooling (at age 16) remains relatively low in England; and the drop-out rate from courses high (7 per cent from A level first year; 17 per cent from Advanced GNVQ first year; 21 per cent from Intermediate GNVQ (Sharp, 1996).

Other OECD countries may not be faring better; indeed, some may be struggling even more to match education and training to the changed needs of employment, technology and the economy.

The search for a more flexible curriculum for young adults

The 1990s witnessed a succession of initiatives in the 14–19 curriculum of which the 1991 White Paper, *Education and Training for the Twenty-first Century* (DES, 1991); The Dearing Review of 1996, *Review of Qualifications for 16–19 Year Olds*; and the 1999 White Paper, *Learning to Succeed: a new framework for post-16 learning* (DfEE, 1999a) were the most significant. These initiatives were in part a reaction by successive governments to changing social and economic forces, both national and global, and the role of education and training in dealing with them.

Coffield (1998b) identified 'a significant silence', however, in government reports, such as the *Learning Age* which gave rise to *Learning to Succeed*, and the Fryer report (1997) on lifelong learning, namely that 'there is no discussion of any kind of the central concept of learning. In all the plans to put learners first . . . there is no mention of a theory (or theories) of learning . . . no learning society can be created without an appropriate theory of learning'. This view is echoed by Silver (1999) when he writes that, 'The research tradition regarding pedagogy has been largely lost in Britain'.

Throughout the twentieth century, educationalists and successive governments were faced with three key questions:

- What should be the age of compulsory education?
- What should the state provide beyond the age of compulsion?
- How best should we cater for the needs of all students in the 14–19 age group, including those who would benefit from a more practical education?

For the first half of the twentieth century the key issue was whether there should be secondary education for all. Prior to 1944, the term 'secondary' applied only to grammar schools which served about 5 per cent of the school population. The 1944 Education Act established secondary education for all, in grammar, technical and secondary modern schools to the age of 15.

The 1944 Act also promoted the legal basis for further education, though there was no clear idea what this would mean. The problems of post war reconstruction were so severe that the implementation of the secondary education programme itself was only slowly achieved. From the middle 1950s onwards the need for a better range of post compulsory provision increased in prominence, and by 1959 the issues had become so complex that the government instigated the Crowther Report, *15–18* (1959), a comprehensive review of all aspects of post-compulsory education. Crowther recommended an 'alternative route' of full time courses for the vocationally oriented student and decisively influenced the development of the further education system.

From the publication of Crowther till the present day, there has been no shortage of government initiatives addressing the second of the key questions in 14–19 education: *What should the state provide beyond the age of compulsion?*

In the 1980s a combination of recession, new technology and a need for greater international competitiveness forced governments of both parties to ask fundamental questions about the contribution of education to the economy. From 1983 onwards, the Technical and Vocational Education Initiative (TVEI) encouraged schools to offer students a more vocationally oriented curriculum, and to involve industry and commerce in both the management of education and its delivery.

By the time of the White Paper, *Education and Training for the Twenty-first Century* (DES, 1991), in which the government announced the introduction of General National Vocational Qualifications (GNVQs), the search for appropriate programmes of full time study for the non-A level student had been going on for almost half a century. The White Paper stressed the government's commitment to maintaining A levels but recognised that many young people want 'to study for vocational qualifications that prepare them for a range of related occupations but do not limit their choices too early'. The White Paper aimed to ensure that high quality further education and training should become the norm for all 16- and 17-year-olds. It laid out the guidelines for GNVQs which should offer a broad preparation for employment as well as an accepted route to higher level qualifications, including higher education. It was the intention that GNVQs be of equal standing to academic qualifications at the same level. By the time of the Dearing Report in 1996 GNVQ was well-embedded in schools as well as colleges. Importantly the principle of flexible curricula, based on units or modules, and outcome statements had become an orthodoxy, leading to change in upper secondary, further and higher education provision.

It is not the purpose of this book to enter into the whole debate about the intrinsic value of the present qualifications structure, the place of A levels, and the operational difficulties of the GNVQ. Other writers have addressed these issues (Hyland and Weller, 1994; Bates, 1995; Wolf, 1995; Sharp, 1998). The status of vocational education as being 'separate but equal' is still predicated on the status of GCE A levels, 'and the standards they represent' and the Higginson report (1988) that recommended fundamental reform of A levels was largely ignored. The Dearing Report (1996) recommended modestly that the term 'Applied A level' should replace Advanced GNVQ, and in February 2000 the Secretary of State announced (DfEE, 2000a) that GNVQs would be re-named 'Vocational A levels' in order to 'raise the status, attractiveness and effectiveness of work-based learning and vocational education for young people'. One of the terms of reference of Dearing was 'to have particular regard to the need to maintain the rigour of General Certificate of Education (GCE) Advanced levels' and the report consistently adhered to this. The universities continue to show that for entry to 'academic' subjects they want high grades at A level; although for 'vocational' or applied degrees many will accept GNVQ/Vocational A levels. It is clear, however, that A levels are the 'gold standard' for English 16–19 education. In other OECD countries too, there are similar academic 'royal roads' to higher education and employment success.

Although the White Paper *Education and Training for the Twenty-first Century* (DES, 1991) was aimed at the needs of 16–19 year olds, there appears for the first time in an official document a diagram of the whole qualifications structure from 13–adulthood which clearly recognises the contribution of the National Curriculum to vocational education (Figure 1.1).

The National Curriculum, introduced in 1988, carried with it the language of standard assessment tasks (SATs) and levels, Core and Foundation subjects, Key Stages and so on. It is not at all clear, however, how the National Curriculum was to play a role in vocational education. *Education and Training for the Twenty-first Century* stopped short of directly encouraging vocational courses in the pre-16 curriculum. Furthermore, it seems ironic that at the same time as the issues of progression and continuity were being expressed in the White Paper, the incorporation of colleges of further education was being planed to take effect from April 1993. This cemented the break at 16 in statute through different funding arrangements for schools and colleges.

The qualifications structure which *Education and Training for the Twenty-first Century* set out, and the whole question of curriculum continuity and progression, is pertinent to the third question posed above, *How best do we cater for the needs of all students in the 14–19 age group, including those who would benefit from a more practical education?*

	General NVQ	NVQ level	Occupationally specific NVQ	
	Vocationally-related Post Graduate qualification	5	Professional qualification Middle management	
Degree	Vocationally-related Degrees/Higher National	4	Higher Technician. Junior management	Degree
A/AS Level	Vocationally-related National Diploma. Advanced Craft Preparation	3	Technician. Advanced Craft Supevisor	A/AS Level
GCSE	Broad-based craftsmen. Foundation	2	Basic Craft Certificate	GCSE
National Curriculum	Pre-vocational Certificate	1	Semi-skilled	National Curriculum

Figure 1.1 General NVQs and the equivalent qualifications. *Education and Training for the Twenty-first Century*, 1991.

The 14–19 curriculum has to be seen in the context of a formal, legal break at 16. All the messages *pre*-16 are about subjects, norm referencing, the bench mark of GCSE grades A–C and the desirability for the most able to enter for the 'gold standard' of A level. The status of a vocational offer within the curriculum has been left to individual schools. Those schools which have explored this widening of the curriculum have, for legal reasons concerning core subject entitlement for all students, used the options proportion of the timetable to include a vocational offer. This compromise is the same as that adopted by TVEI planners in the 1980s. Curriculum 'pathways' in schools vary. To avoid the association of vocational education with education for the less able, some students are offered GCSE options in Engineering or Business Studies. Other, more radical schools, have developed the concept of the *applied curriculum* which includes a variety of opportunities, examples of which are: a link course with a local college; work experience on a regular basis, perhaps a day a week; an enhanced personal and social education programme; opportunities to develop leisure interests which could lead to employment; smaller classes to help with basic skills; and other initiatives aimed at making the year 10 and 11 offer more relevant and attractive to less 'academic' pupils.

By the late 1990s, arguments supporting the availability of a vocational route for pre-16 students had found widespread support. It was possible for policy makers to speak openly about some students not finding the National Curriculum appropriate. The Dearing *Review of Qualifications for 16–19 Year Olds* (1996) endorsed the provision of vocational courses in schools, acknowledging a trend that had been developing in some schools since the TVEI initiative. The review recommended that students should have opportunities to take approved GNVQ units at Foundation and Intermediate levels from 14 onwards. From September 2000, schools were allowed to disapply the National Curriculum regulations at Key Stage 4 so that any pupil could drop up to two subjects in order to follow a more work-related education (DfEE, 2000b). Similarly, provision was made post-16 for schools and colleges to offer more breadth of study. Curriculum 2000, based on modularising A levels, A/S levels and GNVQs/Vocational A levels, is intended to allow students a more flexible curriculum that can combine academic and vocational subjects. Key skills also became a normal part of the curriculum for all learners. These initiatives, however, were not part of a fundamental redesign of qualifications but a repackaging of existing qualifications. Furthermore, schools and colleges were largely free to determine what flexibility they would provide to learners, leading FEDA (2000) to state that 'the capacity of institutions to deliver these opportunities varies and could lead to significant discrepancies across the country.'

The White Paper *Learning to Succeed: a new framework for post sixteen learning* (1999) affirmed government backing for ideas which progressive schools had been piloting in the 1990s. The paper announced the setting up of Learning and Skills Councils, based on the then Further Education Funding Council and the Training and Enterprise Councils, and set out a clear agenda to produce a more flexible curriculum to suit all young people, including the less 'academic'. Two extracts from paragraphs from the White Paper make its intentions clear:

3.18

The Learning and Skills Council must build on the work already done to promote progression for all 14–19 year olds, particularly those who have previously been turned off by learning. Currently, schools have flexibility at Key Stage 4 to enhance opportunities for work related learning. Our proposals for a revised national curriculum from 2000 extend this approach and will provide wider opportunities, as will *Qualifying for Success* reforms announced earlier this year which will increase the opportunities for young people to pursue a broader post-16 curriculum. We want to build on the best practice in schools, further and higher education and work based provision. There should be enough flexibility in the curriculum to allow options for those who are not motivated by a traditional curriculum offering and would find other options, such as the more vocational route, attractive. This will include schemes whereby disaffected and excluded 14–16 year old pupils are able to study in colleges and voluntary sector providers in conjunction with employers.

3.19

We would expect the Learning and Skills Council to seek further ways of enhancing opportunities for young people to be able to study in flexible ways that suit their needs. The Council will do this in part through the promotion and support of work experience programmes for those aged under 16. It will build on the contribution of all those involved in Education Business Partnerships (EBPs), including local education authorities, to ensure coherence between school business links for pre-16 education and the post-16 agenda.

The implications for the practice of teaching, for teacher training and in-service training are profound. *Learning to Succeed* set a target of 85 per cent of young people to attain level 2 qualifications by 2002. Some of these young people, by government admission, will be disaffected and excluded students. This will be a massive challenge to teachers – and to those whose job to it to train them, both pre-service and in-service. Leaving aside the contentious issues of funding, the need to achieve enrolment targets and a host of quasi-competitive dimensions, there clearly are wide pedagogic and operational implications for teachers in both schools and colleges in responding to an increased participation and achievement rate post-16.

In the case of the school sector, even assuming that the courses on offer are appropriate and well designed, there needs to be a sea change in attitude and approach by some teachers if the vocational offer is to be implemented successfully. There are a number of major differences between the pre-16 and post-16 offer:

- Modularised qualifications, with the concept of credit for identifiable assessed learning which can be portable between qualifications, require a new way of managing the teaching/learning process.
- Vocational qualifications carry with them a vocabulary of competence, evidence and verification that affects the teacher–student relationship, which at pre-16 is based predominantly on norm referencing, to one which incorporates some of the features of a criterion referencing approach.
- There is a subtle difference between a curriculum based on 'subject' – what Hirst and Peters (1970) refer to as 'forms and fields of knowledge' and the idea of a 'focussed' curriculum, with the vocational focus being the hub of the wheel and the units like the spokes. The introduction of Curriculum 2000 and the changes to the A level and AS interface are still largely subject driven.
- Delivering programmes of study which meet the needs of students with more practical and experiential learning styles and that, crucially, are perceived by the students themselves to be different and exciting, carries a need for some teachers to adopt different teaching styles.

Colleges of further education also face new challenges to meet the needs of a more diverse student population. Though many colleges would claim that they are very experienced in the delivery of modular and vocationally focused programmes, in managing criterion reference assessment, and in adopting a wide range of teaching and learning styles, the situation on the ground is patchy. For the colleges the concerns may well centre on:

- Students disaffected with education whose study habits are brittle. Some may have chosen to leave school almost at any price. The vagaries of the job market and parental pressure may have resulted in some of them coming to college not entirely out of choice.
- Not all students get on their first choice course, for a variety of reasons, as Bloomer and Hodkinson (1999) have shown.
- Students who have learning difficulties but not so marked that special educational provision has been approved or who have been to a Special school.
- Students with unrealistic expectations of either the more 'open' style of course which they expect in the college or the greater 'freedom' of college life.
- Students who bring baggage from home or their environment which affect their learning. This can also lead to a perception of the teacher student relationship which the student wants to see as distinctly 'non school'.

The role of teachers

Teachers should definitely *not* be blamed for structural weaknesses and policy deficiencies in the British educational system, even though they may appear to be the people most visibly and directly responsible. It has been estimated (Brekelmans and Creton, 1993) that only about 5 per cent of educational attainment is attributable to teachers. Overwhelmingly the most important factor in achievement is *home background* and *previous achievement*, accounting for up to 80 per cent; followed by *student ability level*, accounting for perhaps 15 per cent. This is not to say that teachers are unimportant. The 5 per cent of achievement directly attributable to teachers may make the difference between staying on or not beyond the school leaving age; or going to university.

The effect that teachers have on young people may be as much or more to do with raising their confidence and self-esteem as with imparting subject knowledge and this 'lifelong' process may start at the very outset of schooling. The concept of 'self-esteem' is code for sets of personal knowledge, skills, attributes and understandings. It is argued by Harré (1998) that the idea of a general trait called 'self-esteem' that somehow inheres as part of a person is a reification. What teachers, and others engaged in working with people, should seek to accomplish is to foster a whole range of quite specific knowledges that in turn will boost an individual's confidence and therefore 'self-esteem' in situations where the knowledge may be applied. For instance, a young person may be a skilled footballer and therefore display high 'self-esteem' on a football pitch, but be illiterate and therefore lack 'self-esteem' in other situations. What this person needs is help to maintain and develop their footballing talent and help to become literate. They don't need a class in raising self-esteem. Similarly decontextualised lessons in 'problem solving' or communication are likely to have little benefit, whereas taking a problem solving or communicative approach to learning, in which learning is based on 'real' situations and genuine personal engagement, is more likely to be beneficial.

Managing changes in teaching

According to the 1999 FEFC Chief Inspector's report:

> Strategies to raise performance and standards work best in colleges where there is a strong lead from the principal and the senior management team and where standards of teaching, student achievement and retention are an absolute priority for the team. Colleges in which students succeed are devoted to that end without compromise.

The report emphasised the need to take the training and continuing development of teachers seriously. It particularly recommended the setting by teaching teams of their own performance targets to increase retention and achievement, as part of self-assessment. The report also cautions against seeing learning resource centres as a substitute for effective teaching,

> ... increasing the amount of time students spend working on their own is not a substitute for teaching. It is a means of encouraging students to take some responsibility for their own learning and of making the outcomes of teaching more effective

These recommendations are in keeping with the Fryer Report (1997) on lifelong learning which recommended that,

> The focus of policy and practice should be learners themselves . . . This would shift attention away from structures and institutions, which should be regarded as more or less efficient mechanisms for the delivery of demonstrably high quality learning.

Inspecting teaching quality

During the 1990s the inspection of schools and colleges intensified. The Office for Standards in Education (Ofsted) became responsible for the formal inspection of the quality of teaching in schools and colleges of further education. Similar formal inspection arrangements exist for British higher education through the Quality Assurance Agency. It may be the case that inspection of quality has helped to raise standards of teaching. From an overseas perspective, such as that of the United States with a more fragmented federal system, centralised inspection may appear to be a general good that will help to raise the quality of teaching (Grubb, 1999). Where initial assessment shows that an institution is performing well, it is usual for self-inspection to be instituted.

In most formal inspection or assessment of teaching quality an outsider to the particular course or teaching situation sits in and observes one lesson. Putting aside whether what they observe is normal for the class, it is inevitable that judgements are made on slight evidence. Few schools and colleges in the UK can have escaped the distressing sight of teachers professionally and personally deflated after a summary and negative judgement of their teaching.

Teachers are expected to treat learners with respect and to build their confidence. To judge any human being on the basis of an hour or so in their company is harsh in any circumstances. Even in the best, collegial practice, where someone respected and known to the teacher sits in on a lesson or two, what can be judged accurately? How can friendly stroking of the 'You're doing a great job' variety be avoided? Such stroking may lift the spirits and is very welcome but it may do little to help teachers to improve their practice.

Teaching, as every teacher knows well, is normally a lonely business, which is a paradox because it always involves being with other people. Teachers know how alone you can feel in a room of thirty or more people. It feels as if the focus of attention is on you though in actuality students are usually less focused on the teacher than teachers think. However, teachers are responsible for using this precious time together wisely and for shaping the experience of each individual in the room. Like riding a bike, if you think too much about the process you will fall off. Teaching, like other skilled behaviour, has to be automatic most of the time. We get into habits, some good, some not so good, and through these habitual behaviours we cope most of the time.

To have someone else enter this enclosed world of teaching is an intrusion. The smiles of a sympathetic colleague come to appraise us can do nothing to alter this fundamental fact. And a government inspector, dropped in from some other place, is a most threatening intrusion, even for confident and experienced teachers. After an hour or so, when they have gone, there may be a feeling close to having been burgled. If you are fortunate, the thief will praise some of your goods to you.

The whole shabby business is wrong headed and bound to be ineffective in raising the quality of teaching. Some teachers may ponder aspects of their teaching but whether they can or will change their habitual practices is another matter; others may sigh with relief and smile at the praise they have received; others again may determine to be better prepared to pull the wool over the appraiser's eyes next time they are inspected.

For most teachers to improve the quality of their habitual practices, a number of pre-conditions must be met:

- first, the individual teacher must feel personally responsible for appraising and developing their own practice;
- second, this appraisal should be based on accurate information;
- third, the individual teacher should be supported by others who face exactly the same self-development processes. This must include senior staff, even if they do not teach, because they too use habitual practices that should be appraised in the interest of a more effective education for students.

Personal responsibility

Most teachers do feel personally responsible for the quality of their teaching and few would deny that this should be so. However, there may be a large gulf between the rhetoric of personal responsibility, 'Of course, I am personally responsible for my work. I am a professional', and the actual reality.

A FEDA report on non-completion of GNVQs (FEDA, 1998) found that one of the most important factors in non-completion in the perception of students was the quality of support from teachers, whereas teachers and institutions hardly acknowledged this factor. Only 1 per cent of centres perceived dissatisfaction with the quality of teaching, and only 4 per cent conflict with staff, as among the main reasons for student withdrawal.

Unavoidably, we perceive the world from particular vantage points of age, experience, position, gender, and so on. That teachers perceive that student drop-out from education is because of poor ability or motivation is understandable; and likewise, it is not contradictory that students may blame teachers for a lack of support. One view is not right and the other wrong. They are simply different perspectives on the same circumstances. It is because of the slipperiness of human perceptions that it is necessary to base personal responsibility, whether as teachers or in any other capacity, upon accurate information.

Accurate information

Accurate information about how we tend to teach may be hard to find. Teachers usually work in isolation. Feedback from learners is constant, in the form of their behaviour and their performance and achievement but this sort of feedback is very 'noisy'. It is full of crackle and background static, and it is often difficult for a teacher to stand back and make sense of it. Conversations over coffee with colleagues may tend to emphasise features that really stand out boldly, like unruly behaviour or amusing incidents, but these may shed little light on the normal patterns of teacher–learner interaction and whether these are working well for the benefit of students.

An occasional observation visit from a colleague, especially if this has been prepared for, may also fail to reveal any worthwhile insights into the normal, day-to-day patterns of classroom interaction.

How then can teachers obtain accurate information upon which to base personal responsibility for developing their practice? In some institutions, it is usual to have students complete an evaluation form at the end of a course. This may be useful in planning the next course if it is carefully designed and read by a teacher not for a general approbation or disapprobation but for details of what may need to be improved. Course evaluations are better than nothing, but they are often a long way from providing a basis for self-directed professional development. Students may be constrained by the limited range of questions asked, may fear the effect of negative judgements on assessment, or may focus on important but relatively surface aspects of a course, such as the nature and timing of assessment, or the relevance of content, rather than saying anything about underlying and habitual patterns of teaching and learning style.

Balancing educational inputs and outputs

One reason for government policy and practice over the past 25 years or so to be focused on the outputs of education is because of a belief, implicit in Callaghan's 1976 speech, that teachers and their inputs had become too much the focus, to the detriment of whether the outcomes of education suited the needs of the nation. A great deal of government intervention followed, to specify outcomes and to test these by inspection; however, as we have seen this has not brought about a state in which most people are happy with what is provided. We are flogging the same old educational horse to try to squeeze a better performance but perhaps it is time that the horse was put out to pasture and more fundamental reform introduced.

To restructure education in a way that responds adequately to technological change and its consequences, vulgar pragmatism should be avoided. There are no quick fixes that will bring about reform. Instead:

- The professionalism and experience of teachers should be developed and taken more seriously. You can develop the most detailed and rigorous qualifications and outcomes specifications, but unless teachers and trainers breath life into them they will not succeed. Educational initiatives succeed not in the planning phase but in the implementation phase. Teachers and trainers need to be provided with an adequate language to address their own development needs and the institutional support to change.

- Much more attention should be paid to getting the balance right between the inputs and the outcomes of education and training. Learners who have a successful experience of learning come again and they also spread the word. You can have the most comprehensive and coherent system in the world, but if learners are bored, or if teachers are too busy filling forms to manage teaching and learning, then the learners drop out. GNVQs in particular are supposed to 'promote active forms of learning by requiring students to demonstrate a range of cognitive and interpersonal and practical skills' (Jessup, 1995: 33), but there is too little evidence that this is really happening (see Harkin and Davis, 1996b).

- The entire process of the development of the education and training system should be democratised. Learners have a right to high quality learning experiences, leading to a 'decent' job; employers to a skilled workforce; teachers to be heard on educational matters; and government has a right to intervene to set frameworks and standards, in partnership with all these stakeholders. All these rights carry with them corresponding responsibilities: employers to take training seriously; teachers to take their own professional performance and development seriously; learners to take advantage of learning opportunities by participating actively, rather than being passive recipients; and government should realise that what James Callaghan called for in his 1976 speech at Ruskin College was not government domination of education and training but for a partnership in which the voice of government, and the resources which go with it, may be raised legitimately, in partnership with others whose voices are legitimate too.

The purpose of raising all these wide-ranging issues of technological change and the responses to it of government policy for education and training is to put into context the work of teachers and learners when they come together in education. Teachers have largely to work within the constraints of the world as they find it, and learners are constrained to make choices within the confines of whatever frameworks of qualifications and assessment procedures that the government has approved. Within these constraints, however, teachers and learners between them construct more or less effective ways of working together. Human beings have free agency, even within the sometimes narrow confines of the National Curriculum and post-16 qualifications. There is much that individual teachers can do to enhance individual learner's experience of education. What follows in Chapter 2 is a closer look at three issues affecting the nature of learning: telematics, new insights into learning, and the development of key skills. Thereafter, the book offers teachers a review of ways in which learning may be enhanced, even within the constraints that teachers and learners face. It is possible to develop relatively democratic, co-operative learning practices that enhance students' chances of becoming personally engaged in learning, for its own sake and as a preparation for adult life and employment.

2 Developments that affect learning and teaching

New opportunities for learning and teaching using new technologies

When setting out to research this topic, a librarian was asked to recommend sources of information. The librarian responded by writing down two websites, 'http://www.becta.org.uk' and 'http://www.ngfl.gov.uk'. She assumed that was the way that all teachers would now follow 'cold' enquiries on a new topic. She offered no suggestions for books in stock.

The norm when undertaking research is now to utilise various types of information media, such as computers, the World Wide Web, digital technology, and so on. We live in what has been termed the 'Telematic' age. In fact, the websites recommended by the librarian only produced a few insights, such is the nature of the Web at times. In late 1999, there were about 9.5 million websites; by early 2000, this had grown to over 11 million. According to Taylor (2000): 'Most are dross or just irrelevant but more and more are informed, fascinating and probably just what you need to engage children and students.' Clearly, the practice of using electronic technology is rapidly becoming a very important force in education.

To the librarian, the Web operates like a huge library, with the added benefits of multimedia features. Its 'search engines' and 'indices' and 'key search words' are substantially in the same tradition as library systems of the past which relied on cataloguing and classification systems such as the Dewey Decimal system. When someone wants to find out something in the traditional library, they search the computer catalogue for the location of a journal, a video cassette or a book. If they know with accuracy the name of the object, or its author, or its classification number, the search is simplified. If not, they have to search via the use of 'key words'. The Web is basically similar, if one knows the website one can pinpoint the search more accurately; if not, then key words may help, just like a library.

However, the World Wide Web is more than a library. It is an international communication medium that connects people for a multiplicity of purposes, both for business and socially. All sorts of information and merchandise is available to all who have access; data can be 'downloaded' and incorporated into other files, people can send data to each other or simply 'chat' across the Net; people can manage their finances, take part in auctions or just play games.

Parallel to the computer revolution, and very often symbiotic with it, there are similar revolutions in television, photography, the recording industry, mobile telephones and more, with the arrival of digital technology. In a society such as Britain's, the twenty-first century is an age of telematics and the implications for education are still being worked out. We do know that they have the potential to bring about profound changes to the way that education opererates as people have easier access to knowledge, when and where and in forms that they want.

It is possible, however, to strike a cautionary note. Human thought processes are often iterative; that is, they proceed step by step, sometimes falteringly, sometimes in leaps. The drafting of written materials, like this chapter for example, often requires hard copy that we can read and make notes on, a speed of composition dictated not by the fastest technology but by the dogged progress of human thought. Most PCs have more features than most people will ever use and old fashioned writing and drafting and pausing for thought may be necessary for many people as they form their ideas. Technology provides more or less sophisticated, and more or less useful tools, depending on our purposes and levels of skill at using them. It is the human agent who should determine when technology is worth using, and where it may be a hindrance.

A study by Grubb (1999) of United States Community Colleges included considering how computer technology is affecting teaching and learning. It concluded that technology does not transform teaching and learning but merely reinforces whatever are the current practices. So, for example, if a teacher is highly didactic, presenting lots of information while the students are relatively passive, then computers can be used to present the learners with even more information. If the students are not skilled at processing and analysing information this can be particularly problematic as they face an even greater overload of new material.

Silver (1999), commenting on the use of communication and information technology in education (CIT), including the EFFECTS project in five universities, recorded that: 'The message from many areas of application, however, is now surfacing more clearly that there may have been too strong a focus on the technology and policy directions and not enough on the pedagogical implications.'

Schools and colleges are often poorly funded for books and equipment, so the immediate reality is unlikely to be as glamorous as some views of telematics may indicate. Lewis and Merton, writing in 1997 (BECTA, 1999), noted some of the issues: 'use is patchy; technology is rarely used as a strategy to develop independent learning; the learning environment in which the technology is used remains fundamentally unchanged; teachers lack confidence to make full use of the technology; use is not guided by the results of research.' The sight of students filling in gapped handouts, copying from the overhead projector, using a basic text book to make notes, performing routine manual tasks, completing a simple paper and pen exercise and so on will not disappear from classrooms overnight and such activities are not without value in the right context. The electronic revolution will not be reversed and embracing its possibilities is a major social responsibility for the teacher.

The impact of the telematic age on students

- Many young adults have embraced the world of telematics and have grown used to a 24-hour, multi-dimensional, global view of the world. In their private lives, their social standing and their expression of street credibility often comes through appearing totally at ease with the latest technology. To many of them, the concept of being in a set place for a fixed time, such as a class room, is untypical of the way they organise the rest of their life. They may feel that they are capable of learning when they want to, where they want to and at a time and a pace which suits them. Although most experienced teachers would regard this view as fallacious if taken to an extreme, they are finding that they have to adjust to it to some extent.
- The second implication is that the student body, composed of increasingly electronically confident, some would say dependent, young adults will find it natural in the future to word process all assignments, to file them electronically by subject, to carry disks for school and college as their predecessors used to carry exercise books, and to have assignments set and corrected on disk. All colleges and most secondary schools already have drop-in computer centres and the government in partnership with industry is committed to installing computer facilities in all educational institutions.
- Third, teachers and students alike will be faced with the challenges of keeping reasonably up to date, with problems of maintaining system compatibility, and with constantly changing expectations of access and usage.

Implications of the telematic age for teachers

- In the twenty-first century, all vocational areas are highly computerised. Learners will go into, or are already in, working environments which are computer dependent, so they will need to be confident with all aspects of new technology, which means being much more than merely word processor competent. The effect on teachers therefore, especially those who teach in vocational areas, is an on-going need to incorporate new technology into their teaching and to try to be as industrially compatible as possible.
- Traditionally, teachers have been in control of the existing technology. Now that learners have access to the same technology as teachers, they may wish to set the pace. Teachers will have to develop strategies to harness student enthusiasm and perhaps superior technical ability.
- The future learning environment will be more fluid than that at present and sometimes the students will teach their teachers and fellow students. Teachers will need to adjust to this if they have not done so already.
- Teachers' professional identity will depend less on the fact that they *know*

more than their students and more on their skill in assisting their students to engage more meaningfully with what they are finding out and to help make their knowledge more coherent.

- Though many young adults will have at their disposal a vast array of information and can access it skillfully, others will not have home based facilities or will be less skillful. Access and skillful use cannot be taken for granted, and teachers will need to be as wary of too high expectations as of too low expectations. The identification of Information Technology as a Key Skill in both the Key Stage 4 curriculum and the post-16 curriculum may help in this regard.

- New technology will compel teachers to be more creative and innovative in the way in which ideas are presented to students. Commercially available packages, written to national standards and approved by government, will relieve teachers, if they choose to use them, of some of their instructional role. Interactive programmes are now commonplace. But this approach needs careful planning. Students will not learn effectively just by being placed in front of a computer expected to get on with it. According to BECTA (1999) there must be 'collaborative working between curriculum or subject specialists, library and learning resources staff and technical staff to ensure that all students – whether working within the college or remotely in the workplace or at home – have access to professional support when they need it.'

- Teachers themselves will be able now to create high quality teaching materials which are just as professional looking as those available commercially.

The indispensible role of teachers

Powerful and all pervasive as the new technology is, it is not a threat to the teacher for a number of reasons. First, there may well now be too much information available to learners, so they are likely to need guidance in locating information from a variety of sources; selecting what is appropriate from a mass of potentially useful but confusing data; analysing information from different perspectives; and critically evaluating different types of information. These are key skills, such as those of the national standards for Communication.

Second, the curriculum, however defined, will need to be managed and organised by trained, experienced professionals. Learning is a sequential activity in the same way as time itself is sequential and knowledge and skill would be 'indigestible' without order and logic. Teachers will still be vital to plan, facilitate, mentor and support the learning process.

Third, the capacity of the teacher to respond, sensitively and flexibly, to individual need is irreplaceable. The teacher can change pace, prompt new lines of enquiry, probe for further meaning, deal with misconceptions in a manner and at a speed which no machine could rival. Teachers are sensitive to mood (e.g. confidence, stress, boredom, personal 'baggage', etc.), to the social dimensions of learning, to the subtleties of giving feedback, to the uniqueness of individual learning styles and intelligence. Good teachers see the learner as a whole person, not merely as the embodiment of a set of learning outcomes. Indeed the importance of the new technology to the teaching of young adults lies in its opportunities to enhance the learning process and not in its threats to the teacher's job.

Greater understanding of learning processes

Over the past twenty-five years research has identified further influences on how learning is accomplished and in some quarters these discoveries are being built into the learning process. The idea that the ability to learn is dependent on a single, innate, fixed and quantifiable general capacity of the human mind is strongly challenged by evidence that suggests that learning is assisted or impeded by various and numerous factors. Thus, it is argued, potential educational achievement is not restricted to or even measurable by an intelligence quotient (IQ) but is responsive to an array of opportunities which take into account aspects such as the dominant intellectual capacity and emotional well-being of the learner.

In 1993 Howard Gardner first described his theory of multiple intelligences (MI), defining intelligence as 'the capacity to solve problems or fashion products that are valued by at least one culture'. Working with talented children and brain-damaged adults he perceived that a particular strength or weakness in one area or skill did not predict achievements elsewhere. Further research provided evidence which supported these observations and led him to suggest the existence of not one overarching intellectual capacity but, instead, at least seven relatively autonomous human intelligences: linguistic and logical–mathematical competencies; spatial, musical and bodily capacities; and the abilities to arrive at an emotional and mental sense of self and other people (intrapersonal and inter-personal abilities). Synthesising evidence from biological, cognitive and anthro-pological sciences, Gardner declared that each intelligence has its own pattern of development and brain activity, is essentially genetically pre-programmed with room for flexibility and is different in kind from the others. Consequently the intellectual profile of any one individual reflects the greater or lesser extent to which each intelligence is exhibited, with the make-up of intellectual profiles differing between individuals.

Gardner's approach challenges the very heart of the modern educational setting in the developed world and its view of the learning process. He criticises conventional thinking regarding the existence of a general intellectual competence, stating that the way ability is regarded and assessed is too narrow and that intelligence and competence can be expressed in a variety of ways. Thus from the perspective of MI theory the practice of learning and teaching is confined to the possession and expression of a limited range of skills. The abilities to be literate and numerate are not only the desirable outcomes of education but also the means by which such an education is achieved. For instance, rather than active participation or observation students passively attend to the presentation of abstract materials in symbolic forms; the focus on written language and information technology enables individuals to relate to each other in non face-to-face ways and the influence of the scientific method of thinking emphasises objectivity, systematic investigation and argument. Success in this system requires predominantly linguistic and logical–mathematical skills, mostly ignoring spatial, bodily-kinaesthetic, musical, inter- and intrapersonal forms of intelligence. By promoting some abilities over others, because of their importance in a specific cultural context, many individuals have either struggled in or been excluded from the learning environment.

The notion of multiple intelligences offers a broader concept of the learning process and hope to those who find current education practices restrictive or failing. Gardner's argument implies that the importance and usefulness of an 'intelligence' should be seen in relation to an individual's intellectual profile and subsequently drawn upon to aid the learning process. Differences between individuals' capabilities should be acknowledged, accepted and valued and then used as diverse entry points to stimulate learning and achieve understanding. In this way the wider use of graphical or artistic representations, stories, drama and role play, reflection, discussion and active participation both to explore and express what is learned offers those with different ways of representing the world an option which best suits their abilities and opens up dimensions of learning hitherto hidden from them.

A second dimension of the learning process which has emerged over the past ten years is that of the significance of social skills and functioning for present and future achievement. Various surveys and studies into the relationship between academic intelligence and success in later life indicate that the traditional measurement of IQ is not an unerring predictor of destiny for people with roughly equal promise, schooling and opportunity. Conclusions drawn from such research suggest that IQ contributes at most about 20 per cent to the factors which determine an individual's success in life; 80 per cent is accounted for by other forces such as social class, luck and what is termed by Daniel Goleman (1996) as 'emotional intelligence' or social ability.

Goleman has pulled together mounting evidence which demonstrates that a person's emotional life is every bit as important in determining achievement as are cognitive capacities. New insights into the structure of the brain describe the interplay between thinking and emotion and explain why, at times, passions overwhelm reason, consequently disrupting the ability to think and learn. Longitudinal studies following students through schooling into adulthood point out that those who fare poorly both at school and after are those who, regardless of their intellectual capacities, fail to exhibit a facility with social and emotional skills. His conclusion is that the ability to recognise and handle emotions both in oneself and in others is key to getting on in the day-to-day world. Thus, even with the brightest students their intellectual capacity can become impaired, their ability to learn be crippled and their potential remain unfulfilled if they are unable to control their emotions, manage their life or interact well with others. How much more disadvantaged are those who have only modest or poor academic abilities.

Although some emotions and their attendant emotional responses appear to have been hardwired into the nervous system through evolutionary biology, most emotional circuitry has been and continues to be sculpted and reinforced by life's experiences. This moulding begins in very early childhood, within the context of and shaped by family life – parents and caregivers, through what they say and do, provide a model of how to handle emotions and relationships. In this way individuals learn how to feel about themselves, how others will react to their feelings, how to think about those feelings, what choices they have in reacting to their feelings and how to read and express hopes and fears. But the reality is that many people experience what are essentially dysfunctional relational environments; as a result they fail to acquire an aptitude in emotional intelligence which will help them get on in life and instead need to have access to different ways of reacting and responding. This has lead Goleman to support the moves to 'school the emotions' with regular education aimed at raising the level of social and emotional competence of students in order to equip them to meet the challenges of life.

Emotional patterns can be unlearned, altered or at least controlled, through formal teaching of a more appropriate model which leads to the acquisition and development of more appropriate strategies and behaviour. Since schools and subsequent education establishments are defining experiences that heavily influence individuals through childhood, adolescence and beyond they can do much to address the emotional illiteracy of students. By teachers modelling emotional intelligence themselves, and with the delivery of regular and sustained courses in respect of self-awareness of emotions, self-regulation of emotions and the recognition and handling of emotions in others, new emotional skills can be learned and ingrained to be applied in times of anxiety, stress, frustration, anger or hurt. In this way students are able to develop their thinking capacity to contain and channel their emotions; instead of their cognitive function being blocked by impulsive emotional reactions it is released to concentrate on other things, such as learning. Through gaining social skills and personal control students not only increase their chances to succeed in life after formal education but also are able to focus better on their more immediate academic learning goals.

Implications for teachers of new understandings of the learning process

In one sense, the notions that emotional states and differences in student strengths and weaknesses can impair or enhance learning are not new. For many this may seem to be stating the obvious. However, increasing research evidence is adding scientific credence to what previously were, in the main, intuitive feelings about these matters. It is also prompting a rethink of the structure and objectives of teaching and learning settings in order to meet the diverse abilities and needs of students. For teachers this means becoming more aware of individual differences within a class and providing learning opportunities suited to the way students learn best and not, necessarily, to the way the teacher feels most comfortable teaching. This requires the development of a wide repertoire of teaching strategies, the ability to vary approaches to topics according to student capabilities and emotional disposition, and the capacity to be flexible when something does not appear to be working. A crucial factor in this approach is the need to value the students for who they are, allowing their uniqueness, as much as outcomes, to shape the learning environment and success.

Key skills and the development of the relationship between education and work

The idea that academic and vocational education should be combined, so that people are prepared for life beyond the narrow specialism of a particular job, has been around for a long time. For example, successive reports (Newbolt, 1921; Bullock, 1975; Kingman, 1988) recommended the incorporation of language development across the curriculum. A significant change occurred, however, late in the last century when employers started to call for a widening of the curriculum in order to meet the needs of an economy that had undergone fundamental changes in patterns of employment. Primary industries, such as agriculture and mining, had virtually disappeared in the UK, and manufacturing industry now employed fewer than one person in five. The service sector industries that had boomed, in fields such as telecommunications, sales, insurance, travel and tourism needed different types of skill, more focused upon working with others and communicating effectively. What remained of manufacturing, especially in leading edge, hi-tech manufacturing such as electronics, also required staff who could think for themselves, problem solve and work in teams. The views of a managing director of a hi-tech electronics company, interviewed in the late 1980s (Harkin, 1991), may have been typical. He thought that the trainees he sent to study engineering at a local college of further education learned many things that they did not need to know, or could look up in five minutes in a book. Meanwhile, the knowledge that they did need, such as how to communicate effectively in German as well as English because many of his customers were in Germany, were totally absent from the course.

The Confederation of British Industry report, *Towards a Skills Revolution* (1989) and the parallel Trades Union Congress report, *Skills 2000* (1989) both called for the development of a range of generic or common skills perceived to be needed in employment. In response, the Secretary of State for Education (Baker, 1989) instructed curriculum agencies (NCC, 1989; NCVQ, 1989) to produce reports on the development of core skills (renamed key skills after Dearing, 1996). It was proposed that these skills should not be bolted on to existing curricula but integrated so that learners experience and develop them in real contexts of use.

The original proposal in the NCC and NCVQ reports was for a set of generic skills to be developed as part of all programmes: *Communication, Working with Others, Taking Responsibility for Your Own Learning,* and *Problem Solving*. In addition, there would be core skills in *Application of Number, Information Technology,* and *Modern Foreign Languages,* for people for whom these skills are relevant and important.

As was stated in the last chapter, key skills cannot be developed through didactic pedagogy, in which learners are relatively passive while tutors do most of the talking. These are *process* skills that can only be developed through a process in which individuals practise the skills in their everyday learning and work. Key skills are not free floating and automatically transferable to new situations, but are embedded in specific academic and vocational knowledge, skills and work situations and, in consequence, should be developed *within* learning and work situations, not as add-on extras but as essential and enduring knowledge, compared to the rapid redundancy of much subject knowledge.

In consequence, for example for engineers to have didactic lessons in theory of engineering, divorced from the most up-to-date working practices; quite separately to have lessons in communication is a fundamentally ineffi and ineffective way to learn – yet it is the pattern of much training in the UK contrast, a high-performance company like Volkswagen in Germany appro engineering training as fundamentally about communication. Apprentice together in teams of six drawn from different engineering specialisms; equipped workshops they collaborate to solve real problems, working to six-sided tables to pool their knowledge and skills.

In both the USA and the UK, there is what has been called pragmatism (Grubb, 1996) that leads to re-formulations of outmoded education and training in order to avoid fundamental reform, espe would require employers to play a more active role or education to d didactic pedagogy. Demands for accountability lead to a focus upo and skills that are easiest to teach and to assess; unfortunately, tl and skills needed by an advanced technogically oriented, service which high value added from the human imput is most import difficult to teach and to assess. Skills such as effective communica solving can only be developed in a lengthy process of practice, ir realistic situations. Assessing competence in these areas is com making value judgements, against thoughtful criteria, within d judgements that, to be developmental, must be made ir themselves.

In the UK, there has been universal support for the pr and assessing these process skills, whilst there is almost or resourcing to make this possible. The Further E recommended that in order to develop core skills there management of change; systematic planning and deve lum; learner participation and action planning; the learning opportunities; and regular structured time skills. The recommendations were largely ignored.

Sadly, instead of reforming pedagogy to make c UK government policy tended to reinforce outmode on reform. First, it was decided that only three of *Number, IT*) would become mandatory for some le be optional; second, there are different key sk

learners, depending on their learning programme; third, instead of seeing the key skills as about changing the *process* of learning to one in which learners would become more active and would work *together* to develop knowledge, the skills were seen in the traditional way as a list of competences to be assessed for individual learners. There was no attempt to change the pedagogic practices of the learning programmes of which the key skills were a part and, in direct contrast to declared government policy, the usual pattern of key skills implementation became bolt-on provision.

To make matters worse, the key skills specifications were phrased in the jargon-laden language of all NCVQ documents and needed several re-drafts to become comprehensible to learners and teachers. Nevertheless, they were accepted in principle as a good idea by learners, teachers and employers and, in successive re-drafts, were made more accessible. However, despite national recommendations, there was very little national or institutional support for the development of key skills; the staff teaching them are often part-time and of low status; and the end result is that, at the time of writing, there is little evidence that the skills are being developed as intended, or being assessed to national standards. Typically, vocational programmes continue unchanged; learners are given a little time each week, often set aside at a time that is inconvenient to vocational or academic subject teachers, during which a 'Communication', 'IT' or 'Maths' teacher may work with them in what is largely a decontextualised, 'skills and drills' continuation of secondary school English, IT or Maths lessons.

There has been no serious attempt to reform the institutional and pedagogical practices that make the development of key skills very difficult. Instead, successive revisions to the key skills proposals have made it easier for them to be implemented in watered down ways that do not challenge the dominant curriculum and pedagogy. This is an example of planned failure: the desired change to the process of education is not happening, so the initiative itself is abandoned before the change has had time enough to succeed.

As so many times before, when curriculum reform is proposed that implies fundamental change to entrenched pedagogy, reform is tamed and marginalised. The recommendations of the Dearing Report (1996) have largely been ignored:

> All schools, colleges and training bodies providing education and training for 16–19 year olds . . . should provide opportunities for all young people to develop their key skills and have them assessed and recognised.

> Teachers will need help and guidance through programmes of staff development, to enable them to provide opportunities for the further development of key skills.

There are signs that the DfEE are taking these recommendations more seriously, but a general vulgar pragmatism, involving lack of clarity and coherence in

policies, vacillations and slippage in planned reform, ensures that the endeavour to equip young people with the knowledge and skills they need in order to feel personally engaged in education and training, and to succeed in developing their talents, is thwarted. There is no conspiracy involved, it is just easier to go along with present education and training practices, or to tinker with ideas of using information technology as a quick fix, than to tackle the revolution in pedagogy that is so badly needed if there is indeed to be a 'skills revolution', as recommended by the Confederation of British Industry in 1989.

Implications for teachers of the development of key skills

Many teachers see themselves mainly as subject specialists, and this becomes more so as the age of learners increases. However, many subjects, both academic and vocational, change so rapidly that often motivated students, with access to the latest information via the Web, know as much or more than the teacher. The development of key skills as a discrete part of the curriculum – which is mainly the case at present – may be superseded by key skills as an integral part of learning and teaching. To some extent, this was part of the original intention underlying key skills (Oates and Harkin, 1994) and the intention was expressed by the DfEE (2000c):

> The government is committed to these [key] skills becoming a normal and natural part of post-16 education and training. However Ministers are sceptical about whether the most effective way of promoting these is, in the long term, through discrete units. They see the main value of the specifications in these skills as 'setting the standards'. In the long term the best way of promoting achievement may be to incorporate these wider skills into occupational qualifications.

The implications for teachers are clear – their role is to manage the learning not only of their specialism, whatever that is, but through their work with learners to develop key skills, such as problem solving, taking responsibility for learning and performance, and communication. For many teachers this will present a formidable challenge to their professional identity, as well as to the knowledge and skills that they bring to bear in their work. It was recognised by the DfEE, that even the new, discrete key skills qualification posed problems for teachers, '. . . if the new [key skills] qualification was to succeed we needed to improve both the confidence and competence of teachers and trainers to deliver key skills. This was as true in schols and colleges as in workbased training.' How much more challenging would be the integration of key skills into all learning, in keeping with the need to help learners develop the knowledge and skills that they will need in adult life generally and in employment.

Part II

Theories of learning and teaching

3 What is effective learning?

What learning theorists and psychologists can tell us about effective learning

In much education there is a tendency for learning to be treated simply as the delivery of knowledge and values by those who know more (teachers) to those who know less and know it less expertly (learners). In other words, teachers transmit and learners ingest a commodity called knowledge. This kind of 'learning' as a mode of transmission views knowledge as an entity which is fixed, public, written and formal; it allows the outcome of learning to be treated as a differentially measurable product; it considers teachers to be 'the experts' and views learners merely as receptacles for and disembodied from whatever learning is supposed to be taking place. Consequently, learners are frequently attributed with passivity; are deemed to have little experience and understanding that is relevant to the situation and are seen to have a capability to learn that is likely to respond only to incentives and deterrents. A typical learning experience is likely to consist mainly of a traditional 'chalk and talk' lecture or 'skills and drills' workshop, with little opportunity for students to contribute or exchange views and little possibility to choose topics or learn in different ways. As we know, under such circumstances, learning often does not take place.

Drawing on work from diverse areas of education, clinical and organisational psychology, language and social interaction some idea of what constitutes effective learning can be gained. In summary, as we shall see, successful learning contexts:

- must actively engage the learner;
- are facilitated by social interaction.

Effective learning is a dynamic process

Individuals do not go through life merely reacting, mechanically and without consideration, to external influences. People make choices, choices about how to interpret events, how to respond to situations, what goals to set and how best to achieve them. According to Bandura (1978) these choices are effected by exercising self-regulation – the ability of the individuals to influence their own destiny. People are not only reactive but are also proactive, determining their own direction in life, anticipating the future, in concert with rather than in reaction to any environmental demands impacting on them. This view that humans have agency or power to shape their own existence is central to theories of constructivism and Phillida Salmon (1988, 1995) argues that to be effective educational settings must facilitate learners in experiencing and determining their own understanding and learning.

Salmon considers learners to be active participants in life, constructing their own view of reality and acting upon it. She derives her approach to teaching and learning from the work of George Kelly, a clinical psychologist (Kelly, 1955; Bannister and Fransella, 1986), on Personal Construct Theory. Kelly viewed people as 'scientists' who attempt to predict and control phenomena by developing ways of construing or interpreting the world which are useful in anticipating events. By interacting with the world individuals construct their own knowledge and understanding of reality. They create a network of personal interpretations (constructs) and place meanings on different aspects of life which they then live out day to day. In this way, from the start of life, individuals are proactive, engaging with and making enquiries about what interests and motivates them. Selecting from alternative constructs they categorise events and learn to direct their own behaviour rather than simply responding to external demands.

Consequently, it is possible to treat understanding and knowledge as provisional and never final. For although each individual knows the world and interacts with it only through their own personal construct system, the interpretation they choose to place on any given event is only one of a list of possibilities. In this way, other individuals will hold different constructions of knowledge and therefore, further investigations or information about the world can provide opportunities for personal meaning to be reconsidered and re-construed. An individual's construct system can therefore evolve rather than being fixed. So, through a process of active enquiry, personal knowledge and understanding can be extended or changed.

Since learning is concerned with knowledge – what people know and how they construct what they know – whether, and to what extent, formal education can help individuals to develop their knowledge has been considered by Salmon. More often than not, a transmission mode of teaching results in the mere reproduction of presented material (or surface learning; Gibbs, 1992) – a regurgitation of what the teacher says but which learners may neither understand, hold to be their own nor have any idea of how else it may be used. The alternative of a constructivist mode provides the opportunity for learners to make sense of the material for themselves and to find its relevance to other parts of their lives (deep learning; Gibbs, 1992) – teachers who allow learners to be active participants in the learning process will satisfy learners' natural tendencies for inquisitiveness and promote reflection on and, where necessary, revision of the assumptions by which they live. In order to achieve the latter, explains Salmon, effective schooling must do more than confirm and elaborate taken for granted realities of common sense. It must allow and encourage learners to question, to encounter different experiences, to try out competing understandings, to reflect on and challenge their existing constructions, where necessary or desired to change their position on an issue. In this way, learners will be able to move from 'knowing that' to 'knowing how'. They will also have more opportunity to act in ways suited to life outside schooling and be more equipped to take their place in the world of work. Therefore, effective learning should involve a process where learners can 'come to know' through engaging with and investigating the world, creating and developing their own sense of meaning, assimilating new understandings with what is already known and experienced. This highlights two key aspects of effective learning – it revolves around experience and involves the development of personal meaning.

The role of experience

The challenge then for teachers is how to structure lessons which enable learners to make personal sense of the meaning that the teacher is trying to communicate. The constructs a learner brings to the learning environment are interwoven with personal meaning and value, are frequently implicit and deeply embedded. Any acquisition of new knowledge will entail adjustments to this system and if personal horizons of understanding are to be extended, new learning must be assimilated with what is already known. This was recognised in the early part of the last century by John Dewey (1933) who defined the kinds of experiences and conditions that lead to intellectual development and growth.

Dewey (1963, 1974) believed that the way learning occurs inside the formal educational setting should not be isolated from learning found elsewhere. He advocated a continuity of the process of learning between settings and viewed each student's greatest asset as being their direct, personal experience which must not be ignored or thrown away in this process. He proposed the principle of learning through personal experience which rests on two factors: one internal and one external. First, there is the notion of a continuity of experience in people's lives whereby every experience a person undergoes changes them in some way, and this change, to some extent, alters the quality of the subsequent experiences encountered by that person. Second, there is the idea of interaction in which current and past experiences of humankind impact on the world around, shaping the environment and giving rise to a series of situations in and by which the individual's experience occurs and is touched. These two factors interlink so that although different situations succeed each other, creating new experiences in the process, something from a previous experience is inevitably carried over from one experience to the next. In this way, learning as a process of modification by and of the individual takes place. But as far as education is concerned, as Dewey made clear, whilst learning comes about through experience not all experiences are genuinely or equally educative. Those he considered truly educative are experiences that promote the continued growth and development of the individual and provide momentum for future learning opportunities.

Thus, in his view the task of the teacher is twofold: to evaluate whether the direction of a learner's experience is conducive to continued growth (continuity), and to determine the kinds of situations which are suitable to promoting continued growth (interaction).

The direction of educative learning is judged according to the criteria of self-control and whether or not a student is learning to replace actions based solely on desire and impulse with intelligently considered self-directed behaviour or determination of purpose. Determination of purpose requires the ability to form an end view by taking into account the consequences likely to result from some action. The process demands the operation of the intellect through observing the conditions and circumstances of a situation and understanding the significance of action arising from that observation. Such an operation requires an ever increasing knowledge base, in the form of subject matter (facts and ideas), and the abilities to view, organise, understand, discriminate between and act upon information and ideas that are encountered within the experience. Consequently, if an experience develops the realm of subject matter, intellectual capabilities and is moving an individual to learn to postpone immediate action upon impulse until observation and judgement have intervened, then it is considered to be aiding that individual's growth and development.

The kinds of situations Dewey proposed as suitable to promoting this continued growth are those which exhibit a co-operative community, utilise activity to enhance intellectual growth and give rise to problems that stimulate thinking and development. These are all aspects which Dewey felt teachers could regulate to some degree, and indeed would need to do so, if what a student does is to lead to learning. The role of the teacher is to guide learners to use their intellect and this can be facilitated by the way a teacher uses their knowledge of their learners, activities and subject matter to shape the environment. A co-operative community is conducive to learning through the way it regulates behaviour, allowing attention to be directed towards the activities of learning. By giving students within a group the opportunity to contribute to and be responsible for the process and outcome of learning, both for themselves and their peers, each individual has a stake not just in their own learning but also that of the other group members. Learning becomes a communal affair in which participation in a range of communal activities holds the group together whilst catering for the diversity of each individual. This working together as a social enterprise exerts control over behaviour in a manner similar to participation in games. Conduct in games is regulated by a set of rules and aims to which all participants are agreed, committed and adhere, and within which individuals interact to accomplish their mutually compatible and dependent objectives. It is the same in this social process of education. The locus of control is invested in the nature and aims of the activities in which both teacher and students jointly take part. Consequently, instead of being a controller of behaviour a teacher is released to concentrate on the conditions for learning, becoming a co-participant with their students by helping to select, plan and guide activities that will best create a co-operative community according to their learners' needs.

However, a co-operative community alone is an insufficient environment to promote learning. Simply allowing learners to be involved in creating and managing their own learning through a process of social control which also entails individual freedom can lead solely to wilful and profligate physical activity. Dewey felt that such outward action, directed merely at desire and impulse, stunts intellectual growth since it fails to develop or draw on the capacities of observation and judgement mentioned earlier. Instead of being a means for self-gratification, this freedom of outward action needs to be seen as the means by which freedom of intellect, the development of thought, is attained. For Dewey, directing intellectual development through outward activity can be achieved in two ways. First, such activity leads inevitably to self-disclosure by students as they reveal more of their nature and abilities, affording the teacher an insight into their learners that was not forthcoming when they were merely passive onlookers. Second, the process of active engagement allows a learner to become immersed in experience, an undertaking that can form the basis of reflection during quieter times. So, for the teacher, the new understandings acquired of their students through activity enables the teacher to organise and provide more appropriate and purposeful instruction. For the students, the act of reflection raises their awareness of their experience and helps them to develop powers of observation and judgement and execute deliberate, purposeful action.

This use of experience through activity becomes even more conducive to intellectual development when it progressively leads a student into unfamiliar territory and engages them in intellectual enquiry. Although the starting point of instruction needs to be the experiences a learner already has, the aim is to provide successive experiences that will expand existing learning. The selection and organisation of subject matter needs to ensure a continuity in the line of activity but, at the same time, it should lead students into new areas where unfamiliarity is likely to give rise to problems. For, as Dewey argues, it is the presence of problems or difficulties in learning that stimulates thinking and growth, as ways of dealing with them have to be found by exercising intellect. Problem solving involves: gathering information, facts and ideas; forming objectives; analysing potential solutions and outcomes; making appropriate choices. The overarching ability required is that of organisation, in which the powers of observation and judgement are utilised to consider the way things interact with each other to produce specific outcomes, in the scientific manner of cause and effect. In this way, directing thought towards identifying, analysing and selecting means to reach intended aims turns what would otherwise be aimless activity into intellectual engagement and development. As long as the problems emerge from current experience, are within the range of students' present capacities and arouse a desire to seek further information and produce new ideas, the foundations for further experiences from which new problems emerge are created. Then learning becomes a spiral of enquiry through which learners come to understand and use experience to direct, expand and continue their growth and development.

Dewey offers an explanation and understanding of how the medium of experience enables knowledge acquired every day to be connected with the kind of knowledge found in educational settings, and subsequently expanded. However, for the teacher there still exists the practicalities of engaging with and expanding a learner's experience and interpretation of reality. Decisions have to be made about how to structure learning in order to provide continuity and interaction. Foremost concerns about how to utilise experience in instruction are: what counts as experience?; which experiences should be selected?; and how can these experiences be used to facilitate effective learning? Starting with the last of these, perhaps the best way in which learning can be made more manageable in the eyes of the learner is through the use of learning styles.

Experiential learning and learning styles

Building on the work of Kurt Lewin, Kolb (1975, 1984, 1993) has been a key contributor to the theory that effective learning concerns the reinterpretation and reshaping of experience. This is based on the assumption that people learn best by doing things then thinking about how they have done them, considering both the details of the experience and the thoughts, feelings and perceptions which emerged during the experience. Effective learning is seen when a person progresses through a cycle of four stages: of (1) having a concrete experience followed by (2) observation of and reflection on that experience which leads to (3) the formation of abstract concepts (analysis) and generalisations (conclusions) which are then (4) used to test hypotheses in future situations, resulting in new experiences. Utilising the framework of Lewin's experiential learning models, Kolb chose to label these stages 'concrete experience', 'reflective observation', 'abstract conceptualisation' and 'active experimentation' (Figure 3.1).

This model emphasises learning as an integrated process with each stage being mutually supportive of and feeding into the next. Hence, it is possible to enter the

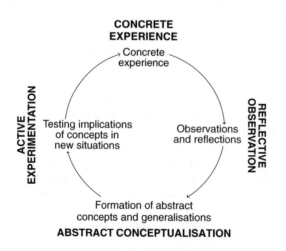

Figure 3.1 Kolb and the Experiential Learning Model.

cycle at any stage and follow it through its logical sequence. But effective learning only occurs when a learner is able to execute all four stages in the model. No stage of the cycle is effective as a learning procedure on its own. For instance, since purposeful activity is not achieved solely through experience and experience is not reshaped by considering only the theoretical possibility of change, an individual needs to be able to move between being an actor, involved in and dominated by experience (concrete experience) and being an observer, detached from, analysing and creating concepts about experience (abstract conceptualisation). Similarly, as a predominance of reflection on experience will inhibit active testing of theories, and constant action and experimentation will preclude the development of thinking intelligently about experience, an individual needs also to be able to move between interpreting the data collected from experience (reflective observation) and actively testing the theories subsequently devised (active experimentation). In these ways, an individual can gain new experiences, perspectives, understanding and knowledge.

However, as Kolb discovered, people rarely draw on all four abilities. Instead he noted four prevalent types of learning styles: converger, diverger, assimilator and accommodator, each one dominated by abilities from adjacent stages in the experiential learning cycle (Figure 3.2). This occurs because, in reality, individuals form preferences for certain abilities over others and habitually use the successful strategies and tactics arising from them to interact with the world. Consequently, a particular approach to learning develops which contains both strengths and weaknesses in relation to the relative emphasis placed on each of the abilities represented in the experiential learning cycle (Table 3.1). So, people come to learn differently from each other and, often, in a way that is not as effective as it could be if every ability were used.

Honey and Mumford (1992) have drawn extensively on Kolb's work and, as a result, there is a great similarity between the two theories. Both views consider experience to be the basis for learning, promote the experiential learning cycle as

Figure 3.2 Kolb's learning styles in relation to the Experiential Learning Model.

Table 3.1 Learning styles as defined by Kolb (1984) and Honey and Mumford (1992)

Style (Kolb/Honey and Mumford)	Learn best
Accommodator/activist	From doing things; from short here-and-now tasks; in carrying out plans/experiments; being involved in new experiences; through trial and error/taking risks; with other people.
Diverger/reflector	When standing back, listening, observing; from collecting information and thinking it through, through different perspectives and grasping the big picture; by sharing and discussing ideas with others; through searching for meaning; with other people.
Assimilator/theorist	When reviewing things in terms of systems, concepts, models, theories; when absorbing ideas and providing integrated explanations/theories; solving problems; by data collection; planning and organising work; through critical evaluation; working alone.
Converger/pragmatist	When integrating theory and practice; in the workshop or laboratory using skills/learning and testing theories and applying common sense; with clear goals and rewards; with things rather than people.

the ideal model for effective learning and suggest that, in reality, people have preferred styles of learning. However, the main differences lie in the way experience is defined, the terminology used and the way this is presented in the experiential learning cycle. First, for Honey and Mumford, what constitutes experience is considered mainly in objective terms of what people do, of being engaged in activity, as opposed to Kolb's more holistic interpretation, which also counts subjective elements of thoughts, feelings and perceptions as experience. Second, the terminology used to describe each stage of the learning cycle and its function is somewhat simplified whilst that used for describing and defining the four learning styles is taken directly from the stage titles. Consequently, the learning styles are positioned around the learning cycle according to their relative stage (Figure 3.3). But the underlying characteristics of each stage and learning style are broadly congruent with those identified by Kolb (Table 3.1).

Learning styles and the experiential learning cycle can be used by teachers to critically evaluate the learning provision typically available to students and to develop more appropriate learning opportunities. First, an understanding of the theory and a knowledge of a group of learners' preferences can be used to help students feel comfortable with learning and to have opportunities to achieve some measure of success relatively easily. This is accomplished by ensuring that activities are designed and carried out in ways that offer each learner the chance to engage in the manner that suits them best. Second, individuals can be helped to learn more effectively by the identification of their lesser preferred processes and skills and the strengthening of these through the application of the experiential

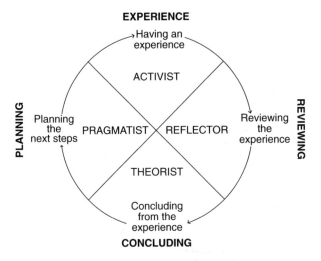

Figure 3.3 Honey and Mumford's learning styles and the Experiential Learning Model.

learning cycle. Third, teachers can assess the impact and implications of their own style on their students and begin to develop aspects that will promote more effective learning. This means that classroom activities should take into account their relative congruence with various learners' dominant styles. Inappropriate learning provision that focuses on only one style to the detriment of others may then be avoided. At the same time, activities and materials may be developed in ways that draw on abilities from each stage of the experiential learning cycle and take the students through the whole process in sequence.

Essentially the theories of experiential learning and learning styles imply that a key to effective learning is the experience of the learner. What exactly constitutes an educative experience is open to interpretation, but what is clear is that the experience of the learner may be utilised by teachers to create numerous ways to engage the learner in learning and make the process relevant to the individual. By encouraging reflection on an experience, understanding can be increased and new things can be attempted. The application of the whole cycle ensures that the individual acquires knowledge relevant to each stage and reinforces the learning that has occurred by making use of it in the next stage.

What is experience?

Dale (1946) saw experience as a compendium of all that happens to us and influences us. All experience in its initial manifestation must enter through one or more of the senses. Dale converted this phenomenon into what he called 'the Cone of Experience' (Figure 3.4). Later, Bruner (1966) provided a way of subdividing these stages into three modes – enactive, iconic and symbolic – representing the forms that knowledge and understanding can take and the order these develop in a person.

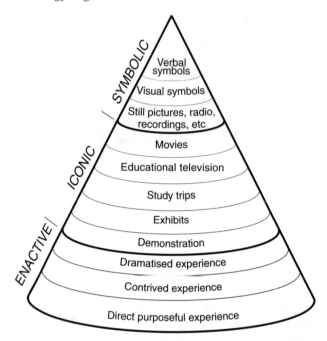

Figure 3.4 Dale's Cone of Experience (Dale, 1946).

Taking the Cone as Dale conceived it and Bruner revised it, it represents a series of relationships which are connected on a continuum from the most concrete to the most abstract. Starting at the base, 'direct, purposeful experience' is the most concrete, active, multi-dimensional, multi-sensory experience which we can have. Such experiences are real. Not only are we present and taking part in some way but the context is 'real': a real game in which we are either playing or spectators, a real meal in a real restaurant, a real job for money and so on. As one's eyes travel up the Cone two things happen: the Cone gets narrower, reflecting the degree of abstraction, and the extent of sensory and active input decreases. As we go up the curve some aspect of our relationship to 'reality' changes, but the situation is still an 'experience'. So a contrived experience is almost real, like a training restaurant, or a training ground, or a simulation, such as a flight simulator; a dramatised experience is a role play which mimics reality but is still role play; and so on up the Cone with decreasing sensory or physical breadth until we come to the most abstract, mono-dimensional, single sensory experiences at the top.

Dale describes the Cone of Experience as follows: 'The individual bands of the Cone of Experience stand for experiences that are fluid, extensive and continually interacting. The Cone uses these separate bands for organising instructional materials according to the sort of experience each provides'. As such the model values and encourages variety and flexibility in what is deemed to be experience and is easily adapted to take into account the change in training patterns and the growth in technological developments and telematics which have occurred more recently. Consequently, we can add to Dale's original list work experience and placements (enactive mode); the Internet, CD-ROM, virtual reality programs and video cassettes (iconic mode) and word processing (symbolic mode).

Dale's Cone is not about intellectual difficulty nor whether ideas from books are more important than those acquired from experience but rather expresses a relationship between different experiences on the continuum. These experiences complement each other, support each other, enrich each other, help to give contextual depth to our life. Consequently, no individual sensory experience is inherently more valuable than another; learning programmes do not have to move from base to apex on the Cone but instead can involve a shuttling process wherein at some stage in the learning all levels of the Cone are used; and the amount of direct experience in a given learning situation should be carefully judged since over stimulus can be as bad as under stimulus.

Dale's analysis deserves wider recognition in the teaching profession than it has been given in recent times. In showing that experience is not a simple or indeed single concept but is in fact multi-faceted, Dale's Cone signifies the relationships between the various media used in teaching and their effect on students with different learning styles and different intelligences. Thus, when a teacher makes a strategic decision to start with the general and work towards the particular (or vice versa) or to move from direct to indirect experience, this not only affects the optimum structure for a particular topic but also the impact of experience on the students. By using the Cone of Experience teachers can enhance their understanding of what can constitute experience and how different experiences can be interwoven in order to add appropriateness, interest and to further the thinking skills of the learners.

Dale's work gives the teacher tools for a more sophisticated use of experience. But how does a teacher deal with the common problem in teaching of how to get across basic facts, concepts, and ideas in a student centred way with as much active involvement of the learner(s) as possible? Naturally academic students, such as those whose preferred learning style is in the bottom hemisphere of the Learning Styles cycle, may not find this too much of a problem. But for those students who favour the top hemisphere of the cycle, the engagement with theory is often a difficult process. For a learner to become more effective in processing information a teacher needs to take into account that managing facts, concepts and ideas is dependent on three interacting forces: the data itself (what is taken in through the senses); an organising framework (which facilitates and holds the whole process together); and inference (the questions asked of the data and conclusions drawn from it). The way this can be achieved is through the application of a procedure devised by Taba (Eggen *et al.*, 1979), also known as the Integrative Model (Eggen and Kauchak, 1988).

Taba's model, which can be depicted as an 'egg timer', consists of seven structured steps or phases covering the data and inference elements of information processing which are connected through a separate organising framework or data retrieval chart (Figure 3.5). The first three phases are concerned with finding out

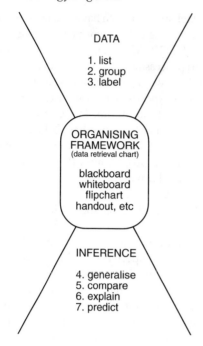

DATA

1. list
2. group
3. label

ORGANISING
FRAMEWORK
(data retrieval chart)

blackboard
whiteboard
flipchart
handout, etc

INFERENCE

4. generalise
5. compare
6. explain
7. predict

Figure 3.5 Taba's Model depicted as an egg timer.

what students already know or have experienced about a topic; this is usually accomplished via a whole class 'brainstorm' or questioning session where the learners volunteer their thoughts in response to something suggested by the teacher. Next, their responses are recorded and, subsequently, challenged with the use of supplementary evidence as the teacher moves into phases 4 to 7 to enable them to draw inferences and conclusions.

The key to Taba's model is the kind of questions framed by the teacher. These are crucial because they determine the types of activity and processes the students engage in. If well thought out, the questions will guide students sequentially through the process of forming generalising, explanatory or predictive inferences at the same time as the activity progresses. But equally important is the teacher's ability to use the organising framework effectively to hold students' ideas, knowledge and opinions. The top and bottom of the 'egg timer' are wide representing the breadth of human experience (data) and human imagination (inference) but the centre is a narrow, finite and fixed shape (in reality often rectangular: whiteboard, handout, etc.) into which the shared data is funnelled and stored. This bottleneck is important as it brings together the variety of student activity and is one device whereby learners can visualise their shared collection of facts, ideas and concepts.

As it stands, teachers utilising Taba's model can enhance their strategic options to enable student experience to be used as an aid to more sophisticated thinking. But by extending the model teachers have in their possession a more versatile and powerful tool to facilitate learning (Figure 3.6).

It is suitable for students of all learning styles but is particularly beneficial for those who are Experiential or Activist learners since it builds on experience by incorporating the more analytical skills of the other learning styles. This can be seen if we relate the model to the experiential learning cycle (Figure 3.7). Data collected in the early phases becomes the source of experience and, through the inference phases it is transformed into ways of reflecting and planning. In this way learners are taken full cycle and are helped to develop and extend their higher level thinking abilities.

Data			Organising Framework	Inference			
1	2	3	Data retrieval chart	4	5	6	7
list	**group**	**label**	**whiteboard**	**generalise**	**compare**	**explain**	**predict**
collect	sort	categorise	overhead projector	distinguish	contrast	analyse	evaluate
find	rank	name	flipchart	conclude	connect	imagine	criticise
choose	sequence		handout	theorise			
bring	match		tables				
underline			columns				
highlight			matrices				
tick			models				
			grids				
			charts				

Figure 3.6 The Taba Model.

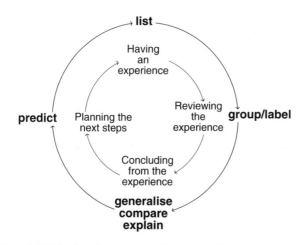

Figure 3.7 Taba in relation to the Experiential Learning Model.

The development of personally meaningful learning

In the early part of this chapter, we stated that experience is one of two key aspects of effective learning to emerge from work based on personal construct theory. The second of these aspects is the development of personally meaningful learning. Studies show that learning may be conceived as consisting of two hierarchical levels: one which reproduces something and another which makes sense of something. The former restricts learning to bringing about an increase in knowledge through memorising, the acquisition of facts and the development of skills and methods to be used as appropriate. The latter makes sense of information, constructs meaning, relates information to every day life and comes to an understanding of the world by transforming knowledge (Säljö, 1979, summarised in Banyard and Hayes, 1994: 303–4). Personally meaningful learning is represented by the second level. However, most students only ever approach or experience learning at the first level, impairing their abilities to build on experience, relate facts, draw inferences and make conclusions leading to purposeful action. In order to move them from the first level to the second, teaching strategies need to be aimed at fostering the development of understanding. Work by Gibbs (1981, 1992) and Rogers (1983) show how this personally meaningful understanding can be stimulated.

Deep and surface learning

By building on the work of others Gibbs has done a great deal to identify ways of influencing the quality of student learning and to provide teachers with an understanding of how their role and assessment methods are key to this. His view on personally meaningful learning derives from the conceptual framework of surface and deep approaches to learning (Marton and Säljö, 1976; Entwistle and Ramsden, 1983; Entwistle, 1987), which reflect the differences between trying to reproduce subject matter and to understand and apply knowledge. If a student reduces what is to be learned to the status of unconnected facts to be memorised, then a surface approach is adopted. If the student attempts to make sense of what is to be learnt, then a deep approach is used. Although a surface approach can lead a student to achieve an outcome, it fails to equip them with a full understanding of a concept or topic, the ability to infer principles from examples, formulate critical arguments supported by appropriate evidence, integrate items into a structure or relate new ideas to previous knowledge or to areas outside the subject matter. Consequently, those who take a surface approach are shown to gain lower marks, have poorer results and are more likely to fail.

Some students are able to use both approaches in their learning, varying it according to their intentions and the nature and demands of the task in hand. Others only ever take a surface approach, for two reasons. First, they are unable to make a distinction between the meanings underlying deep and surface approaches and consequently fail to comprehend the breadth of the concept of learning. Second, characteristics of the course (e.g. a heavy workload, high class contact hours, excessive amounts of course material, a lack of opportunity to pursue subjects in depth, a lack of choice over subjects and study methods, threatening and anxiety-provoking assessment systems) often reinforce, rather than extend and change, their habit and perception. However, it is possible for a student's approach to learning to be changed. To do so course design, teaching methods and assessment need to embody aspects that encourage a deep approach. Gibbs (1992), citing Biggs (1989), highlights four such key elements: motivational context, learner activity, interaction with others and a well structured knowledge base (Table 3.2).

To be effective these elements need to be incorporated thoughtfully into a program of learning. In a project funded by the Council for National Academic Awards, Gibbs (1992) monitored and reviewed innovations designed to improve the quality of student learning. From these case studies he outlined nine strategies which, through the use of various teaching methods, can foster a deep approach to learning.

1   Independent learning.
2   Personal development.
3   Problem-based learning.
4   Reflection.
5   Independent group work.
6   Learning by doing.
7   Developing learning skills.
8   Project work.
9   Fine tuning.

Whilst each of these, to a greater or lesser extent, comprise the four key elements associated with deep learning; simply using the strategies may not have the desired impact on the depth of student understanding. It is also crucial that the

Table 3.2   Elements that promote a deep approach to learning (Biggs, 1989, cited in Gibbs, 1992)

1. Motivational context
Intrinsic motivation is crucial and is developed by students learning something that matters to them; being able to exercise choices in what they learn; being allowed to plan their learning; being in a supportive environment.

2. Learner activity
Engagement in activity, planning and reflection enables connections to be made with previous learning and between new concepts.

3. Interaction with others
Meaning can be negotiated and ideas manipulated more easily with others in discussion than alone.

4. A well-structured knowledge base
New concepts can be understood if previous learning has been well structured, clearly displayed and interrelated.

assessment criteria support a deep approach to learning. Through the case studies Gibbs concluded that the way students tackle learning is dominated by what they perceive they need to do in order to pass and obtain good grades. This perception is gained from an assessment system which often overtly rewards a surface approach to learning. Instead of encouraging attention to meaning and the development and application of concepts and ideas, conventional assessment isolates and reinforces learning as the acquisition of knowledge, the ability to memorise and the use of skills and procedures. End of course assessment methods separate performance from the process of learning, strengthening the notion that what matters is being able to demonstrate a quantifiable increase in what is known; work that requires reproduction of facts or assignments which rely heavily on the use of procedures reduce the need to provide explanations and display an understanding of what is going on and how things relate to each other. For meaningful learning to occur, assessment must be congruent with the use of a deep approach to learning. Approaches that fulfil this objective include involving students in designing the assessment (thus increasing motivation and ownership of learning); devising tasks similar to 'real world' situations and problems (requiring activity and the integration and application of knowledge) and employing assignments which involve students working together (pro-moting interaction). Consequently, when a student perceives the system to be rewarding a deep approach and penalising the alternative, then there is more incentive to adopt the former.

The freedom to learn

In the construction of personally meaningful learning the role of the learner is at the heart of the teaching and learning process. A deep approach to learning is fostered when the conditions encourage a student to learn independently rather than be reliant on a teacher's directives. The role played by the teacher in this contrasts with what is normally associated with traditional teaching, requiring different emphases and skills. The teacher needs to be concerned with how particular processes engage students in learning. The content covered and presentation of the material is secondary to organising learning opportunities and supporting students in learning for themselves. The skills required for didactic teaching need to give way to being able to brief students appropriately for a class-based activity or independent group work; to design assignments that enable students to make sense of their learning; to comment on student reflective activities in ways that promote further reflection; to engage in discussion rather than lecture; to select, provide and ensure access to appropriate resources to support the learning process, to set the learning climate by being empathetic, trusting, accepting towards the learners. As a result the teacher becomes a facilitator rather than a controller of learning and students become directors of their own learning.

For Rogers (1983) it is precisely these compositions of the roles of teacher and learner that lead to effective learning. He defines personally meaningful learning as something that is significant to the learner, discovered by the learner, through the learner's own experience, thoughts and feelings. This occurs under conditions where the learner is personally involved, has initiated the involvement, self-evaluates the experience according to their own criteria and creates meaning by drawing on all aspects of the experience. For formal education contexts to mirror these, students need to be given freedom to responsibly direct their own learning and to be free to be themselves, calling on their own diverse previous experience, interests and curiosity; exploring issues in ways best suited to them individually and actively participating in deciding what is to be done as a class and individually. Students, on entering the education system, have the facility to approach learning in this way. The prerequisite basic elements – the abilities to become personally involved, to initiate investigation, to determine success and achievement, to comprehend different aspects of a multi-dimensional experience – are put in place during early-life interactions with and explorations of the world. Consequently, in order to provide for personally meaningful learning formal education needs to use and build on these abilities. Instead of a prescribed curriculum, similar assignments for all students, lecturing as the mode of instruction, standard tests for the evaluations of all and instructor chosen grades to assess achievement, students need alternatives such as those in Table 3.3 that allow them to create, guide and evaluate their own learning experiences. Through the use of these methods students will learn to responsibly direct their learning and come to gain clearer and deeper insights into themselves, to perceive for themselves what they can do to contribute to or resolve situations, and be empowered to take action, solve problems, become life long learners.

Table 3.3 Methods of building freedom to learn (Rogers, 1983)

Use and build upon problems or issues that are perceived as real and relevant by the students and to the course.

Imaginatively provide all kinds of resources that can give students experiential learning relevant to their needs.

Develop learning contracts – allow each student to negotiate jointly with the teacher the objectives, duration, format, resources, evaluation, etc.

Divide the class into two groups – one self-directed, the other conventional – where some want freedom and others prefer instruction.

Divide the class into small groups and encourage each person to facilitate and contribute to the learning of the whole group as well as themselves.

Encourage inquiry by posing problems and then allow the students to investigate and make autonomous, self-directed discoveries.

Provide short programmes of instruction, based on experiential learning, which students can use when they wish to fill a knowledge gap.

Set up encounter groups – small groups with no preconceived structure – and allow the group members to determine the function and purposes under the facilitation of a leader.

Use self-evaluation to enable each individual to decide what criteria are important, what goals are to be achieved, the extent to which goals have been achieved.

Rogers argues that learning is a whole-person activity combining logic and intuition, intellect and feeling, concepts and experience, ideas and meaning. It is a process which requires the learner to draw and reflect on every facet of their being, highlighting strengths and weaknesses. It is challenging since it involves the learner in reinterpreting and reshaping their experience and coming to terms with the objective or subjective changes to their reality. Hence it is an activity that some learners feel better equipped to tackle and more comfortable with than others. Some are inclined to withdraw from the experience altogether. However, those who feel less sure about their abilities as learners can be encouraged to build confidence, take risks and accept the freedom to learn, if they feel themselves valued as individuals. This requires the interpersonal relationship between teacher and students to be based on interaction, co-operation and openness, emphasising respect, understanding and support. This happens when the teacher becomes learner centred, accepting the students, trusting them to be responsible, empathising with their struggles, nurturing their creativity and interest, and becoming a co-participant with them in the learning process. In this way a climate is created that is positively supportive of students and their efforts to learn, providing encouragement and a safety net as they engage in the discovery of something new and significant for themselves.

Obviously, however conducive the learning environment may be, not every student is willing to take responsibility for directing their own learning. Nor is it always possible to create the kind of opportunities that will maximise the potential for personally meaningful learning for those who wish to have the freedom to learn. Rogers recognised these things. However, if individuals are to become responsible, equipped for a life time of living and learning, they need to be able to inquire and evaluate for themselves. To be able to enter into dialogue and discussion, to deal with affairs of the world or complex matters that affect them, to recognise the pros and cons of each situation and solution, to make their own choices or take a stand on issues, they need to be able to draw on previous experiences. The educational system is one of the places where people should be given a chance to develop the facility to determine, for and by themselves, what shall be learned.

Effective learning is facilitated by social interaction

Clearly, learning is not separated from the learner, their personal situations or their relationships. Although a construct system holds meanings which are personal to an individual, these meanings do not exist purely in a private world. As Bandura (1978) states, whilst an individual is proactive in the environment, the individual is also influenced by environmental forces; shaped by situations as well as being responsive to them; influenced by the behaviour of others as well as being an influence upon others. Variables of differing natures – biological, psychological, physical and socio-cultural – all impact on the course of learning and the effect of each cannot be ignored. However, perhaps the most crucial of these variables in effective learning is that of social relationships. Individuals live, not in isolation from others, but within a society and culture which they make their own in order to belong, take their place and live out their adult lives. As they grow, they become aware of social values and priorities, cultural norms and conventions. They become aware of other people's interpretations of events, competing realities and alternative constructions. All of these have to be met and negotiated, choices made, actions taken. Learning consequently has its basis in the relationships which exist between people. Two key guides to understanding the place of social interaction in learning are by Vygotsky and Bruner.

The zone of proximal development

Vygotsky's (1962, 1978) theory claims that individuals' mental activity, ability to think and reason by themselves and for themselves, is the result of a process mediated by language. Language is seen both as a sign for and a tool of psychological activity and development, but the process in which it functions is, as we shall see shortly, social in nature. During childhood, an individual translates the symbolism of words into meanings and, initially, uses language to communicate overtly with others. Subsequently, the use of language develops also as an instrument to tackle problem solving and to guide and regulate their own behaviour and actions. This occurs firstly as overt or egocentric speech and later becomes inner or internalised speech. With this progression of language use from purely communicative and social speech to include self-directing, internal dialogue, an individual's thinking is also transformed. Thus language and thought become interlinked as the ability to use abstract verbal concepts allows the conceptualisation of alternative and increasingly complex constructions and meanings. These, in turn, provide opportunities to acquire new understandings and insights, new ways of interpreting events and planning for future actions.

The development of an individual's language, thought and actions are fused together only in the milieu of social interaction. From the start of life, an individual's progress occurs within a context which is organised, watched over and influenced by others – initially parents, care-givers and siblings, within the family setting, subsequently by teachers, instructors and fellow pupils in formal educational settings, and later still by employers and colleagues in work settings. Through interactions with these people, development proceeds from the social arena to the individual sphere. In the beginning, a child constructs word meanings from understanding the speech of others; depends on others to support, nurture and share in their efforts to achieve successful outcomes; allows others to introduce thinking and acting in more complex ways in order to master new skills and competencies which were previously unattainable. And it is this working collectively on an activity under the guidance of a more expert or adept person, either adult or more capable peer, that Vygotsky felt is the key to successful learning, at any stage of life. Through noticing that a child often achieved with assistance more than could be done alone, he posited the notion that intellectual progress needs to be based within social interaction and led by instruction which is set in advance of present abilities, awakening and stimulating the various thought processes that currently only operate with interaction. By collaborating with other participants in the learning process, the formation of new concepts can be guided by using language to abstract new elements and traits, and synthesise them with existing meanings and ideas. In this way, cognitive growth can be realised as the individual moves through the zone of proximal development – the measure of learning potential which exists between a person's present development level and that which they are able to reach with the aid of the interactional process. The fact that Vygotsky did not see this view of learning being restricted to mother–child interactions or forms of early learning is due to his insistence that many individuals fail to develop the ability to produce genuine concepts, even during or after adolescence. Instead, tasks and learning currently beyond our capabilities are approached with elementary forms of thinking and require the assistance of more capable others to help bridge the gap between unaided and aided competence.

Scaffolding

Bruner (1966) extended Vygotsky's work on social interaction into the realm of formal education. Viewing learning as a cultural as well as a communal activity, Bruner considers that through a process of communicative interaction with others, individuals make knowledge their own within the community of those who share and engender their sense of belonging to the culture. Thus, Bruner sees the object of schooling as that of helping individuals to share and jointly create culture, considering the educational experience as one which ought to reflect the forum nature of society and prepare the young for life as it is lived outside the school environment. Through the use of language, a dialogue between the various participants of the school experience must be opened up to help them negotiate meaning, to create or constitute knowledge, and indeed, to provoke them into moving through the zone of proximal development, in order to equip them for membership of the adult society. Consequently, Bruner considers that instruction should shape growth in a manner which is complementary to the way learning occurs outside the educational context and which is particularly well illustrated by the processes involved in the parent–child interaction, as suggested by Vygotsky.

To facilitate formal learning in this way, Bruner (Wood *et al.*, 1976) uses the term 'scaffolding' to indicate one way in which structure can be brought to a learning situation within the zone of proximal development. The intention is for learners to engage with a teacher (the more competent adult) in order that each student's thought processes can be stimulated to nurture ideas and enquiry and encourage competency. Through this interaction, which develops through a process of prompts and pointers from the teacher, a learner is facilitated in the organisation and mastery of their experience. As the learner constructs or extends current skills and knowledge to develop higher levels of competence and control the support provided by the teacher can be slowly removed. Eventually the learner gains sufficient confidence and ability to investigate and develop their own ideas and direct their own learning.

This method of cognitive development proposed by Bruner is heavily dependent on the guidance of the teacher, whether this is provided through question and answer sessions, step by step learning or the use of student experience and active learning methods. But more recent research shows that when the whole process encourages learners to engage with each other to construct their knowledge, it is equally effective (e.g. Light and Glachan, 1985; Gauvain and Rogoff, 1989). When learners collaborate with peers, being permitted to talk about possible solutions to problems and to engage in practical actions needed to test potential outcomes, intellectual development takes place. It is argued that this is due to the communicative nature of these interpersonal relationships – working together, dialogue, discussion, argument – which helps stimulate enquiry and enables alternative constructions of knowledge to be shared or created between learners and a consequent different reality to be established.

Relevance of theory to teaching young adults

The theories covered in this chapter cover a wide range of learning scenarios, from primary age (Taba and Bruner), through secondary schooling (Salmon), undergraduate learning (Gibbs and Rogers) and work place learning (Kolb, and Honey and Mumford). Little has been derived from work directly involving young adults – those in their mid to late teens; in fact, no theories of learning are known to exist specifically for this group of learners. However, this does not make the propositions put forward here either irrelevant or inappropriate. On the contrary, what can be seen is that the key elements for effective learning are the same across the whole spectrum. Experience and the need for personal meaning as the bases for learning and the facilitation of learning through social interaction are found at each level. There is, therefore, every reason to suggest that such elements are equally vital for effective learning for young adults. Consequently, taking these into account when planning for and reflecting on teaching and learning is essential to promote successful learning and confident learners.

4   The role of students in effective learning

Meeting the needs of students

Young adults live in an age of social turbulence. For those in adolescence, the passage is often difficult to steer. Particular features of adolescent angst are not new but they have been made more prominent in literature, film, popular culture and in society in general since the 1950s when the term 'teenage' was coined.

Not all young adults are adolescents but it is important to consider some features of this transitional period in people's lives. Horrocks (1976) identified six points of reference in viewing adolescence:

1   A time when an individual becomes increasingly aware of self in the form of the idealised self or self-concept.
2   A time of seeking status as an individual.

> There is a tendency to attempt emancipation from childish submission to parental authority and usually a struggle against relationships with adults in which the adolescent is subordinated on the basis of inferiority in age, skill and experience. It is a period of emerging and developing vocational interests and striving towards economic independence.

3   A time when group relationships become of major importance in terms of status, and often conformity to the actions and standards of peers.
4   A time of physical development often idiosyncratic to the individual and a revision too of the body image.
5   A time of intellectual expansion and development. 'S/he is asked to acquire many skills and concepts useful at some future time but often lacks immediate motivation'.
6   A time of development and evaluation of values. 'It is a time of conflict between youthful idealism and reality'.

Much of what Horrocks identified in the 1970s has resonance for the twenty-first century but life for the adolescent today is very different from that of their parents. Teachers attending a training course identified these issues that adolescents today have to face:

Issues faced by adolescents

- Drugs
- Acquired immune deficiency syndrome (AIDS) and human immuno-deficiency virus (HIV)
- Early exposure to adult issues through the media
- Media pressure through advertising
- Lack of clear moral framework
- Differentiated legal ages for sexual intercourse, smoking, car driving, entitlement to free education, etc.
- Homelessness
- Sexual abuse
- Dysfunctional family life
- Lack of parental authority
- Inner city problems
- Computers and new technology
- Transport in rural areas.

It is not an exhaustive list. Some of these issues existed in the 1970s but the perception of the teachers was that the pressures on young people are now much greater than they were. Boundaries seem blurred, rights of passage more diffuse, horizons uncertain.

Identity

Questions of identity, which have always troubled adolescents, have become more difficult to resolve. According to Josselson (1994), 'Identity represents the intersection of the individual and society. In framing identity, the individual simultaneously joins the self to society and the society to self. . . . In adolescence, young people first confront the challenge of finding a place for themselves in the larger social world'.

If the adolescent lives in an area where none of the adults are in full time employment, or the employment pattern of parents has been irrevocably broken within the adolescent's lifetime, or the social fabric of the neighbourhood has changed, finding an identity in the larger social world can become very difficult. 'The work environment, broadly conceived, tends to dominate most of our waking moments, and sometimes our occupational identity is seen as *the* defining characteristic of the self' (Raskin, 1994). Many young adults face a future where their identity through work will be uncertain.

If what is seen as 'work' appears unattractive or uncertain or just different then the option offered and approved by both government and society is to continue in education for an extended and, what seems at 16 or 17, an indefinite time. For those who take a full-time vocational course there is no guarantee that it will lead to a satisfying job; for some who choose A levels the postponement of the need to take on a vocational identity leads to a time in limbo – the end seemingly too far away to seem real.

Complex societies that offer wide choice make (more or less) available to young people a moratorium in which it is understood that choices are tentative, playful perhaps, and not for keeps. In this period, the young person is (more or less) free to explore ways of thinking, being, doing, and valuing that might fit.

Josselson, 1994

She goes on:

In our society, college offers such a moratorium. The young person is free of the necessity to be taken too seriously and allowed to make mistakes and to investigate belief systems, relationships and occupational choices while society (in the forms of parents, teachers and friends) regards the proceedings with bated breath.

Most teachers like to feel that they relate well to adolescents and most probably do. Catan and colleagues (1996) showed that the normal pattern of relationships between adolescents and adults is mutually respectful and supportive and does not support the stereotype of moody and troubled teenagers who could be living on a different planet from their parents and teachers. However, Catan's work also shows that there are communication breakdowns, particularly among more vulnerable groups of adolescents, such as off-site secondary pupils, unemployed and homeless young people. Similarly, a study of non-completion of GNVQs (FEDA, 1998) showed a general satisfaction with teachers but a marked dis-satisfaction by students who had dropped out. They cited lack of teacher support as one reason for their failure to stay the course. Teachers cannot take for granted that young adults will regard them in a positive light from their perspective and experience.

Life history

All learners carry with them the cumulative effects of their life history. Life history for young adult learners includes their life experiences, their long-term aspirations, life's successes and failures, and their strengths and limitations. If a subject or a topic which we teach is inherently difficult for some learners to under-stand, it is often because of their life experiences. Teachers either compound that experience in a self fulfilling way or they can use their expertise and training to adjust their teaching to accommodate to the life history of each learner.

Anyone with a reasonable training and aptitude for the job can teach students who are competent and interested in the subject. It is far more demanding to teach those whose life history is of failure to understand and failure to be understood. For students whose life history and experience of education has been unrewarding, it is important to be given a chance to reposition themselves as learners. If their views, skills and existing knowledge are valued, this can make a major contribution to the learning process.

Life history is the starting point in working out how best to motivate students. Young adults need support in the transition to adulthood. Knowles (1970) says, 'as a person matures, self concept moves from dependency towards self direction'. It is important that the effect and value of each individual's experience is built into the teaching and learning process. No one's life history is likely to show a universally well-motivated profile. The work for example of Kolb (1984), Honey and Mumford (1992) and Gardner (1993) demonstrates that individual differences in learning styles affect what we are good at and what we gravitate towards. Many studies (e.g. Bernstein, 1971; Banks, 1976; Halsey *et al.*, 1980; Holtermann, 1996; Cohen and Long, 1998; Ball, 1998) have demonstrated links between social class, family values, child rearing practices and educational progress. In short, we know that educational achievement is likely to be as much the product of environmental factors as of any innate tendency to a particular learning style or type of intelligence. Nevertheless, people do learn in spite of natural or environmental disadvantages. Something inside themselves makes them wish to succeed. This phenomenon is called *motivation*.

Theories of motivation

Newstead (1998) took the view that motivation, not ability, is 'the crucial determinant of how students approach their studies and of how well they perform'. Motivation is a topic of great interest to the teacher. All teachers recognise what it feels like to work with students who are or become well motivated but exactly what this means is difficult to define. Motivation is defined by Greenberg and Baron (1993) as 'the set of processes that arouse, direct and maintain human behaviour towards attaining a goal'. Mitchell (1982) identifies four common characteristics which underlie the definition of motivation, which are that it is *individual, intentional, predictive* and *multi-faceted*.

Historical perspectives on motivation

Motivation is a complex and multi-faceted concept which has inspired many theoretical approaches. It is beyond the scope of this book to produce a thorough critique of them, however, what follows is a brief review of some of the key theoretical bases of the term and an evaluation of their significance for teachers of young adults.

Early studies of motivation in the Western intellectual tradition were concerned with establishing a method of studying motivation which was both scientific and respectable. Prior to the late nineteenth and early twentieth centuries, the dominant explanations of human behaviour were couched in religious terms. Behaviour was shaped according to the word of God interpreted through the Bible with its notion of sin and man's fall from grace, or via some similar religious set of propositions. The laws of the state were associated with the will of God, oaths in court were sworn on the Bible, the conventions through which most Western societies were regulated had their immediate origins in the dominant religion.

The study of psychology in the early years of the twentieth century was very much about academic credibility. Psychologists sought explanations of human behaviour which were more measurable than those in the Bible. Animal studies were used to produce a clinical environment that appeared to be objective, replicable and controlled. In studying how animals behave in controlled conditions, it would be possible to construct theories which would be scientifically 'respectable'. One could précis this view as, human beings are animals and therefore subject to similar influences.

'Drive' theory was one such theory which was viewed as scientifically respectable. What motivates all animals is an innate compulsion to behave in certain ways, according to Child (1993). He differentiates between 'drives', which he defines as innate biological determinants of human behaviour that are activated by deprivation and 'motives' which are activated by social considerations. Drive theory is based on the concept of homeostasis. The body of an animal, and this includes humans, likes to rest in a state of balance and contentment. Only when the balance is disturbed, for example through hunger or sexual needs are we impelled to act. Proponents of drive theory have reduced the reason behind all activity to a form of drive reduction. Psychoanalysts, notably Freud, developed similar views on what makes us behave as we do. Drives according to Freud are said to come from the 'id' and are forces which are subconscious. According to Freud, aggression and libido in particular are the source of many actions if we could factorise all the interconnections.

Drive theory explains many specific human actions but fails to explain why we behave in ways which delay gratification. These require a different term, motive. Again according to Child (1993) motives are learned influences on human behaviour that lead us to pursue particular goals because they are socially valued. The notion here is that there are some aspects of human endeavour where the inspiration to behave in certain ways is inherently governed by values which others share or can relate to. Freud views this as the 'super-ego'. The reward is not a return to homeostasis, which is essentially a static if not passive mode, but the desire to improve or develop the quality of life. It would explain, if one believed it, ideas such as beauty, democracy, philosophy, mathematics, music – indeed the whole legacy of the ancient Greeks. Huczinski and Buchanan (1985) express this notion thus: 'We get pleasure from eating, drinking and breathing but this is not enough. We also get satisfaction from exploring, learning about and influencing the world around us'.

Child summarises the difference as follows:

Drives	*Motives*
Are innate	Are learned
Have a physiological base	Have a social base
Are activated by deprivation	Are activated by the environment
Are aimed at satiation.	Are aimed at stimulation.

These two aspects, drives and motives, are the basis of much of our current thinking on motivation. They were refined by Moorhead and Griffin (1992) as need deficiencies and goal-directed behaviours.

Need theories of motivation

The basis of all need theory is that human motivation is caused primarily by deficiencies in one or more needs or perhaps categories of need, depending on which theory one adopts.

Abraham Maslow

It is thought beneficial for our general well being that we need to have experienced in the broadest sense the warmth and security of a balanced and loving childhood. Abraham Maslow (1943) did a lot of work in the 1940s and 1950s on the notion that successful attention to general needs and the power of positive support at key stages of early development forms the foundation for successful learning at later stages in life. Figure 4.1 represents the Maslow hierarchy of needs.

Maslow is talking about an ideal model which is difficult to quantify but has been highly influential. It has been debated thoroughly in most standard books on organisational behaviour. Some of these are represented in the bibliography so we will limit our criticisms to that found in Huczinski and Buchanan (1985):

> There are two main problems with Maslow's theory. First, it is difficult to see how it can predict behaviour. The amount of satisfaction that has to be

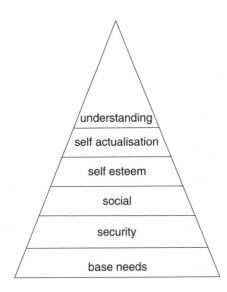

Figure 4.1 Maslow's hierarchy of needs.

achieved before one may progress from one step to the next in the hierarchy is difficult to define and measure. If we could take measurements, the extent to which different people emphasise different needs would make our predictions shaky. Second, Maslow's theory is more like a social philosophy than a psychological theory . . . It is not clear, however, whether the 'higher order' needs (beyond physiology and safety) are innate or learned.

Maslow's value to teachers of young adults is that learners carry life's 'baggage' with them, some of which motivates and some of which demotivates. Statements such as 'I'm no good at learning languages' or 'I could never do Maths' are as much about life history as about learning styles or ability or environment. When teachers come up against demotivated students often they have to deal with the fact that the learner has already had an experience which has been negative and that to change the motivational 'set' of the learner to one where at the very least the young person will have a go at something, the teacher may need to reactivate a generalised 'Maslovian' approach to provide an experience through which learners can feel safe and confident in their own strengths.

Maslow's value to teachers of young adults lies in the fact that hierarchy can be implemented in any learning environment. Figure 4.2 is a visual representation of how the model can be of self-evident value to teachers.

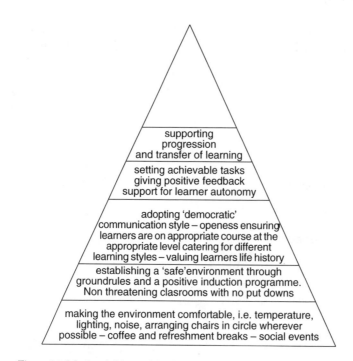

Figure 4.2 Maslow's hierarchy of needs adapted for teachers of young adults.

Herzberg's two-factor theory

Frederick Herzberg and his associates developed the two-factor theory in the late 1950s and early 1960s. They interviewed approximately two hundred accountants and engineers in Pittsburgh. Herzberg asked them to recall times when they felt particularly satisfied and motivated by their jobs and times when they felt particularly dissatisfied and unmotivated. He then asked them to describe what caused the good and bad feelings. (Herzberg, 1968). Herzberg had expected to display his findings as in Figure 4.3. In the event, he came up with the model in Figure 4.4.

Herzberg's theory gained popularity quickly and it also attracted criticisms: the sample was small and unrepresentative; these factors vary from individual situation to individual situation; it explains the link between dissatisfaction and motivation better than that between motivation and satisfaction.

Herzberg's two-factor theory is included here not just for its historical curiosity value but because learner motivation too can be influenced by 'hygiene' factors as well as through achievement, recognition and the intrinsic interest of the subject itself. Most teachers are only too aware of the demotivating effect of substandard or outmoded accommodation and facilities; a computer network crash resulting in 'lost' work; shortage of materials; promised modules or opportunities which do not happen, and so on.

satisfaction ---------------------- dissatisfaction

Figure 4.3 Herzberg's two-factor theory in simplified form.

satisfaction   **no satisfaction**
      motivational factors
- achievement
- recognition
- the work itself
- responsibility
- advancement & growth

dissatisfaction   **no dissatisfaction**
      hygiene factors
- supervision
- working conditions
- interpersonal relationships
- pay & job security
- company policies

Figure 4.4 Herzberg's two-factor theory.

McClelland and the need for achievement

David McClelland (1961) identified people who need to be successful at whatever they do – high need achievers – and this motivates them to succeed. According to McClelland, only about one in ten Americans possess this attribute, but he and his associates felt that people can be trained to acquire it through the power of positive thought. It begs the question why should one wish to succeed at everything (often seen in highly competitive behaviour associated with the will to win), and whether this comes as a result of nature or nurture.

McClelland's value to teachers of young adults is as a reminder that some learners are motivated by a desire to succeed which transcends all else. Some of them respond to a well managed competitive learning environment which should not be to the detriment of other learners who hate competition. It is a difficult balancing act but business is all about competition, not to mention the scramble for university places, so the need for achievement can be a clear motivational option.

Goal theories of motivation

Social psychology developed in response to an increasing interest in how different communities and social structures produce different patterns of behaviour. What is the link between motivation and social values? This is a fascinating area of study well beyond the scope of this book and the main reason for including reference to it here is to reinforce the fact that all learners, but particularly young adults, are part of and subject to a complex network of social structures which affect the way they behave and the strength of their motivation to learn.

More recently there have been a number of theories on motivation, developed in industry, that may help the teacher to explain motivational issues in their teaching. Mullins (1999) warns that 'the search for a generalised theory of motivation at work appears to be in vain . . .. It is because of the complexity of motivation, and the fact that there is no ready-made solution or single answer to what motivates people to work well, that the different theories are important to managers'. For 'managers' we argue that one can read 'teachers', since teachers are in a sense 'managers of learning'.

Expectancy theory

According to Moorhead and Griffin (1992), Victor Vroom (1964), 'is generally credited with first applying the theory in the work place. The theory attempts to determine "how individuals choose among alternative behaviours"'. Expectancy theory states that the strength or 'force' of the individual's motivation can be expressed in the following equation:

$$F = E \times V$$

Where F is orientation to behave, E is the expectation (subjective probability) that the behaviour will be followed by a particular outcome; and V is the valence (value) of that outcome.

Porter and Lawler (1968, in Mullins, 1999) saw much subjectivity in words like 'performance, valence, satisfaction' and in the techniques needed to 'measure' them. What is cause and what effect? One example they use is that 'job satisfaction is more dependent on performance than performance is upon job satisfaction'.

Despite the problems of subjectivity, most teachers can think of examples where the equation works in full and the learners are happy with both process and outcomes. But there are countless examples in education where expectancy theory, which is essentially about subjective reaction to particular life experiences, brings about an expectation of failure or irrelevance which gradually erodes the will of the individual to engage in learning. Clearly, if life history has lead to a learner's low expectations or low achievement, or if learners are unable to see the value of the task in proportion to the effort likely to be needed, or perhaps both, then the force of motivation will be very weak. We have to be prepared to *graft* new experiences on to existing healthy and fruitful experiences. Outcomes in the early stages of a learning programme need to be achievable and perceived to be of immediate value if they are to motivate some learners. The immediate value may simply be that they are fun to do.

Job enrichment theory

Huczinski and Buchanan (1985) state that the origins of this theory come from America in the 1970s. They cite five core dimensions to this theory:

- skill variety
- task variety
- task significance
- autonomy
- feedback.

These core dimensions induce three psychological states critical to high work motivation, satisfaction and performance, namely: *experienced meaningfulness, job satisfaction* and *performance*.

The applications of job enrichment theory to teaching are obvious, especially in the domain of vocational education and training. Teachers need to ensure that what they teach is made relevant to the learners and that the methods of transmission are varied. They also need to transmit how much they 'trust' their learners and give them responsibility, and let the students know how well they are progressing.

Equity theory

Mullins (1999) states that, 'equity theory focuses on people's feelings of how fairly they have been treated in comparison with the treatment received by

$$\frac{\text{Outcomes (self)}}{\text{Inputs (self)}} \quad \text{compared to} \quad \frac{\text{Outcomes (others)}}{\text{Inputs (others)}}$$

Figure 4.5 The equity comparison.

others'. It was initially articulated by Adams (1963). The individual first evaluates how the organisation is treating them. Next, the individual develops an evaluation of how a 'comparison-other' is being treated and compares self and other. The other can be a colleague, someone in a similar role in another part of the organisation, or a composite of several people. The equity comparison takes the form of Figure 4.5.

Adams suggested six common methods people use to reduce inequity:

1   We can change our inputs, i.e. work less hard.
2   We can change our outcomes, i.e. strive to increase pay or responsibility.
3   More complex, we can change our perception of ourselves, e.g. realise that we are not as valued by the organisation as we once thought.
4   We can alter our perceptions of others, e.g. they may actually be working harder than we are.
5   We can change our comparative other, i.e. we may have chosen the wrong comparison for a host of reasons.
6   We can leave the situation.

Equity theory has been the subject of much research especially about the manipulation of specific variables such as pay, conditions, posts of responsibility. The value of equity theory lies as much in the review process of organisational culture as the effect of specific changes.

There are parallels between business and education and training. Learners are affected by the ratio between effort and outcome and they naturally compare these ratios with those of other learners, especially those who are perceived to be less conscientious. Flash points can occur over missed deadlines, grades which are too subjective, poor attendance, or failure to comply with requirements, such as some learners not giving an oral presentation when you have done one, and so on.

Students whose view of their life history is one of inequity will quickly react to unequal treatment. It does not matter in their eyes whether the inequity is real or imagined, it will lead to demotivation unless tackled openly. Moorhead and Griffin (1992) make the point that, 'everyone in the organisation needs to understand the basis for rewards. If people are to be rewarded more for high quality work than for quantity of work, that fact needs to be communicated to everyone'.

Responding to both needs and expectations in learners

One other way we can categorise needs and expectations is into *extrinsic* and *intrinsic* motivation, defined by Mullins (1999) as *social* and *physiological*, respectively.

Mullins differentiates between 'tangible', extrinsic rewards and 'psychological', intrinsic rewards. In education and training we would see intrinsic motivation as the impact of the learning process on the learner related to achievement, interest, feeling valued and so on, whereas extrinsic motivation relates to the skill of the teacher in manipulating such things as test scores, competition, rewards and sanctions, fear of failure, variety of teaching method and so on.

Developing learner motivation and participation

All learning involves a relationship between confirmation and challenge. This can best be expressed in the form of a continuum as shown below:

Confirmation ◄─────────────► Challenge

Confirmation in this context means the recognition that the learner's previous experience and preferred learning style are valid in their own right and within the context where the learning is taking place. The life history of the learner is valued and utilised: looking for skills or experiences which have an associated relationship with the learning at hand; using the existing skills of learners to develop new knowledge; looking to capitalise on instinct and even misconception to further understanding.

By confirming or perhaps affirming that we have accepted both the validity of the learner's previous learning and the appropriateness of their learning style, we are signalling a learner-centred attitude which boosts the learner's confidence to continue with learning.

Challenge, on the other hand, needs little amplification. It is human nature to want to accept a challenge. Progress is proportionate to a realistic level of challenge and most people will face a challenge as long as it seems attainable. In the best relationships in education and training, the responsibility for identifying challenges comes as much from the student as from the teacher, though it is the latter who traditionally has set the challenges.

Challenge in relation to confirmation

Although we lay great stress on the need to make the learner feel comfortable in the new context in which they are engaged, there are dangers in operating at the extremes of the continuum. Too much confirmation and the learner might be understimulated. It is common to hear students say, 'Been there, done that' or 'Not another project' or, woundingly, 'That's boring' when we have been too cautious in exposing them to new concepts and ways of working. But if we set the challenge too high then the reaction is just as likely to be vocal, 'Surely you don't expect me to do that!' or take the form of an opting out in the guise of displacement activity, disruption or lack of effort and commitment.

So, the skills of managing the continuum of confirmation and challenge lie at the heart of the teacher's professionalism. Teachers do not stay at a fixed point on the continuum when developing a new aspect of learning but guide the learner through a continually shifting and shuttling process. It is sometimes appropriate for teachers to make a bold expression of a challenge if all the factors suggest that this would be effective, but learner-centred education and training is more likely to be effective if the usual starting point is before the half way point on the figure below, at least in the introductory phase of a new topic.

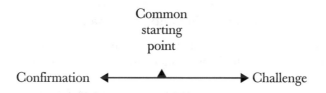

Common
starting
point

Confirmation ◄—————————► Challenge

Using and building on prior knowledge

All data is taken in initially through the senses and as a first filter the brain has a clear choice at the cognitive level: do I recognise this data? The brain searches for a place where the new data can lodge comfortably. Once the first filtering process, often subconscious, has taken place, then the task of training people in the strategies of processing information is essential for continued success as independent learners. Cognition, according to Piaget and Inhelder (1966), involves *assimilation*, encoding information into existing mental files, and *accommodation*, altering existing mental files and creating new ones to take on board new knowledge.

There is much value in planning learning experiences which draw on the widest range of learner experience and knowledge, as shown in Chapter 3. Cognition (thought) is only one of the factors which influence learning. One person's logical thinking can be another person's straitjacket. If students have had unsatisfactory learning experiences it does not necessarily follow that there is something deficient in their ability to think. It could be that they have been expected to accommodate to new ideas through teaching and learning methods which were not natural or beneficial to them.

We still expect our learners to adapt to new environments which is not always easy for them. We can assist them by getting them to draw on skills and experiences already developed and by carefully structuring the learning process. Some of the early skills such as recognition and labelling, classification, the forming of rules, understanding concepts and so on are common to all learning regardless of age. It is likely that a 7-year-old and a 57-year-old will go though similar processes when they first learn word processing. All learners have to assimilate and accommodate to new data and new ideas and all teachers may need to present some new ideas by moving from the concrete to the abstract; from the known to the new.

Active learning

Active learning is a multi-faceted concept. From one dimension, it can be viewed as the opposite of *passive* and that would make as good a starting point as any.

There are things we learn despite ourselves, subconsciously, unconsciously, accidentally, incidentally. I go to the cinema ostensibly to watch a film for entertainment purposes and I learn something about the horrors of a concentration camp or the power of forgiveness and reconciliation. I did not intend to learn anything of the sort but I did. I learned despite myself – I could not help it. There are others who have closed their minds to new ideas so they block out the new learning. Phenomena can be perceived in the physical sense but not internalised. Nevertheless, some form of unconscious learning takes place in all of us. In fact, the act of wittingly engaging in the processes of learning is only a minute part of my whole existence. Even in school, 5½ hours a day plus, say 2 hours homework, for 5 days a week is a small fraction of a child's week.

In the range of methods of teaching and learning which teachers employ, some will be inherently passive. It is unlikely that all students will be equally keen on all lessons every time they go to class. Sometimes they will put themselves in a passive state by shutting out the import of the lesson and in a sense go through the motions. This is not to say that no learning takes place but that their state of engagement is passive. This may well be compounded by the actions of the teacher, as we have already seen, where the style of the lesson sees transmission as the dominant activity rather than the inculcating of ownership and the confirmation of the student's own contributions.

Passive learning occurs when learners are confined to a reactive rather than a proactive role. Typically, they do things such as listen to a lecture, take notes, reproduce a diagram from an overhead projector, watch a demonstration, read what they are told to read, watch a video as the lead activity and then perform some sort of associated activity. The teacher organises and mediates both the structure of the knowledge and its extent and then the student may or may not become actively involved. If the teacher performance, for whatever reason, is not good (and no one can be good all the time and even less so at, say 4.00 p.m., after having delivered two or three lessons already that day!) then the chances of the student sustaining interest is diminished. Yes, 'good' students will learn but not all classes are filled with able, well motivated students. The teacher is active and may well feel drained but the learner may not be.

Passive learning in this context occurs where the learner's role is to be lead. The learner is socialised into taking on board the teacher's structure, and expected to behave in a set way which conforms to the teacher's view of desirable behaviour, so that the teacher can claim that the class has achieved set learning outcomes. This is not in itself undesirable. We have already demonstrated in Chapter 3 that learning is complex and much of what we later come to internalise arrives almost by accident.

Principles of active learning

Any teacher will agree that students need to be given work to do, to be 'stretched' at best, or at worst to be kept occupied. Exercises to consolidate learning, notes to ensure that students can learn independently, say for homework, tasks which check on learning are indisputably the stock in trade of education. There are also many, many examples to be found throughout the world of excellent teacher-centred lessons where the students' interest is maintained by a skilled practitioner, though even the best cannot remain inspiring on demand. But the term *active* goes beyond concepts of showing interest through compliant behaviour.

Stenhouse (1971) argues that there should be some part of every lesson where the students or a student comes up with an idea or an answer which the teacher has not anticipated. If we accept the exponential growth of knowledge throughout history, then this philosophy is worth examining. How should the teacher plan for unpredictable responses, or at least not wholly predictable ones? What instructions should be given to the learners? The teacher needs to be clear on what is expected of the learner.

A learner can be considered to be active when one or more of these elements is built into the learning process: that they are creating something new, or solving a problem or using tools or equipment through 'hands-on' experience. These terms need expanding:

Creating: there are many examples of students creating new artifacts in art subjects, poems and essays in English, designs in technology and so on. There are also examples of students interpreting data in new and original ways, scientific as well as historical. Creating as such is well embedded into education and may emerge even from more conventionally taught situations. But 'creating' is used here in the additional sense of active engagement.

Solving: solving also utilises learner experience and gives a sense of ownership to the learner but, whereas the act of creating involves a new product or a new way of behaving, solving involves the decision making process itself.

Different teachers use solving for different purposes. In actual or simulated vocational situations, such as a training restaurant or a training hairdressing salon or a college farm or similar, there are 'real' problems to solve, 'real' customers to serve, actual working environments to cope with. Other teachers have created assignments whose very nature invites students to solve problems through meeting deadlines, working in a team, locating and selecting information, working out the sequence for a series of actions and so on. Solving involves teachers thinking out one or more 'trigger' verbs which will impel the learners to make decisions and actively engage with what the teacher wants them to do. Teaching as defined by the notion of didactic teaching should be the last resort, as it invites the student to adopt the passive mode.

Hands-on experiences in the context of active learning simply means becoming competent and confident with tools, technology, situations, often vocationally relevant. It qualifies as 'active' because to become familiar with new tools and processes involves several domains of human intelligence, such as both the cognitive and the psychomotor.

One key question for every teacher at every phase in the learning process is:

'*What will the learners be doing?*' If the teacher can think of any way of making the learner active it will enhance the quality of the learning. One example here will suffice to make the point, though there will be others in Chapter 6. If the teacher asks students to read one or two sides of A4 (this could be an article or a short extract from a course book, or a handout) and does not accompany this by an active task instruction to direct the reading, then the results are likely to be indirectly passive. Students can avoid being engaged in the reading or in questions which the teacher may pose, forcing the teacher into more energy to reinforce what should have been read. But if, in setting up the reading, the students are instructed to 'highlight or underline no more than *six* key words or phrases and then share your thoughts with the person next to you', then the reading is task focused and becomes one of solving in addition to one of reading. The student has to make a choice and to discuss this with someone else who has perhaps made a different choice. The student is therefore given the opportunity to rehearse the learning before the teacher poses questions.

There are pressures on teachers to produce students who will achieve high grades, but to obtain high grades students are expected to produce some original ideas or at least some arguments which are not entirely predictable or run of the mill. If this is required in examinations, then learners need to be given opportunities to engage in the process of thinking and arguing during class time. Higher grades are likely to come about when the learner is *active* in one or more of the ways mentioned above. Similarly, the development of key skills, such as communication, working with others, and taking responsibility for your own learning requires that teachers create opportunities and build expectations that students will learn to learn autonomously. The preference of some teachers for teacher-centred approaches may lie both in an attitude to the process of learning itself and to a need to feel in control. A learner put into the passive mode may be perceived as less knowledgeable than the teacher and therefore in need of being taught rather than their learning being facilitated.

Conclusion

We have all heard teachers praise classes that are well motivated or that have a high number of 'intelligent' students, by which is often meant that they are confident in handling abstract theory and academic conventions. It was a 'good' group is often an accompanying accolade to such students as is the corollary a 'bad' group given to students who do not work in the ways which the teacher approves and often epitomises.

Teachers who review their understanding of motivation theory, who manage the confirmation and challenge continuum and display a commitment to active learning principles will have a positive effect on the performance of all their students and not just those who have learned how to perform the 'good' student role.

5 The role of teachers in effective learning

Teachers are professional communicators

Teachers are professional communicators. As Stubbs (1976) put it:

> . . . a person cannot simply walk into a classroom and *be* a teacher: he or she has to *do* quite specific communicative acts . . . social roles such as 'teacher' and 'pupil' do not exist in the abstract. They have to be acted out, performed and continuously constructed in the course of social interaction.

Teachers are aware of this. In 1999, sixty-one practising teachers in further education who were beginning a Certificate in Further Education course were asked to identify up to five characteristics of a 'good' teacher. The most frequently cited characteristic was *good communicator* (twenty-three), followed by *good listener* (eighteen). Other similar characteristics cited were *rapport* or *empathy* with students (fifteen), *approachability* (eight) and *sense of humour* (eight). Only eight teachers failed to list at least one of these constructs.

Effective communication is, however, something that we tend to take for granted. We are born as language users and may assume that, as teachers, we are well equipped to communicate. In a general sense this is true. Three-year-old children are skilled language users, able to equivocate and to make subtle distinctions. Very young children know that you never call a baby ugly in front of its parents. Every adult knows how many pitfalls there are in human communication. Mutual misunderstandings are a feature of much adult interaction and familiarity, as divorce courts know, does not always enhance communication. Teachers may be blind to aspects of how they tend to communicate with learners, and learners too may fail to consciously realise how they are perceived by teachers. Self-perception is so often at variance with the perception that others have of us and teachers cannot escape a fundamental human condition.

It is important that the training of teachers incorporates knowledge of the processes of interpersonal communication that lie at the heart of effective learning and teaching. This may be the case in some training courses, but not all. Is it not surprising that professional communicators should not be trained to communicate?

New learners, new needs

As student numbers grow, new demands are placed on teachers. Not all students are highly motivated to learn and different students may make different demands on teachers. French research (Felouzis, 1994) has shown that three broad tendencies may be identified:

- 'academic' students who are motivated by interest in the subject and who wish teachers to light up the subject in interesting ways;
- 'vocational' students who wish to learn but at the same time who have greater emotional needs and wish for a mutually respectful and warm relationship with teachers;
- and students who are relatively disaffected from education, who may not have done well so far, and who tend to prefer a relatively strict, disciplined environment to help them regain lost ground.

In England, many GNVQ students require constantly to be energised, a process that can be exhausting for teachers, especially as resource constraints mean shorter course hours, larger class sizes and longer teaching hours. The retention of students who are poorly motivated, in order to achieve national education targets, may place further demands on the energy of teachers. At least two surveys (NFER, 1994; NATFHE, 1995) showed that there is widespread stress among teachers.

Negotiation with students is more prevalent in GNVQs than in other programmes, especially when dealing with the demanding evidence requirements. Here is an example of an episode between a GNVQ Health & Social Care teacher and her class:

Teacher: Those of you who haven't put that assignment in, when are they coming in? *(Hand to chin. Smile)* Is there any chance you can get them to me by Wednesday? *(Hand to forehead in gesture of weariness; eyes closed)* Even Wednesday afternoon, last thing. It would give me a chance to have a go marking them and I'll do my best to mark them for moderation on Friday. If you can get them to me by Wednesday. *(Smile)* Yes? There's your friend. *(Smile. Pause. Looks serious and makes eye contact with Peter)* What do you think, Peter?

Student: Yeah, I'll try but *(Silence)*.

Teacher: Well, do your best *(Nose twitched in expression of encouragement)*.

When teachers of A levels become members of GNVQ teams, they often have difficulty in adjusting to this more affective mode of professional behaviour. A level teachers may concentrate more on subject delivery, while learners on GNVQ programmes express a need, through their interpersonal behaviour, for teachers to relate to them more.

Studies in Holland by Brekelmans and Creton (1993, 1994) showed that teachers become less able to display warmth and are more inclined to display control behaviours as they become more experienced. This is unsurprising, given that teachers grow further apart from learners in age and become increasingly familiar with their subject, making it more difficult to understand the conceptual difficulties of learners. The understandable but almost certainly erroneous belief that learners are not as bright now as in the past is widespread; as usual, two-thirds of perception is behind the eyes, however, this does point to a need for continued professional development. Even within GNVQ programmes, that are designed to encourage student autonomy, Bates (1997) found that when students do not demonstrate high levels of commitment, the tendency of teachers is to reclaim control of student learning rather than, for example, to help the students to learn the skills to take responsibility for their own learning.

The training of teachers

All teachers in maintained schools in the UK have to be trained to national standards and the creation of a General Teaching Council (GTC) in 1999 may give efficacy to the concept of teacher professionalism. The White Paper, *Learning to Succeed* (DfEE, 1999) gave support to the training of all lecturers in the further education sector, by use of the Further Education National Training Organisation (FENTO) standards. In higher education, the creation of the Institute for Learning and Teaching (ILT), and the creation of a Higher Education Funding Council centre for pedagogy, indicated a growing emphasis on teaching standards and learning processes. It is important that teachers in all sectors of education are given appropriate training to carry out their work.

Of course, the creation of written national standards does not automatically lead to improvements in the quality and availability of education for teachers; nor does high quality teacher training automatically lead to improvements in student learning. Factors such as the form and quality of training, particularly for serving teachers; and whether new practices may actually be implemented in schools and colleges through senior management support for change determine whether professional development makes a difference to education practice.

Participation in a course of teacher training may give rise to significant improvements in the performance of teachers, at least for the duration of the programme. Teachers on an in-service training programme were perceived to show greater leadership, and were more helpful, friendly and understanding, and were less uncertain, dissatisfied and strict than other teachers. However, it is unclear how long these benefits last. More work needs to be carried out on this topic but there is a strong case for emphasising the need for updatings and refresher courses, especially for teachers who have been in service for many years, and more especially at times of intense curriculum change.

Eraut (1994) has shown how Berliner's five stage model of professional development, from novice to expert, invokes a need for less emphasis on initial training and more emphasis on continued professional development, and is a useful model on which to base realistic professional development. Brekelman's work (1994) shows that it should not be assumed that experience automatically brings progression to higher levels of the Berliner hierarchy. Teachers can become habituated to ineffective practices, and teachers and learners can get caught up in ineffective complementary behaviours.

A study of teaching in Community Colleges in the United States (Grubb, 1999) has shown that, despite a strong rhetoric that teaching is important, senior managers usually have little understanding of the quality of teaching in their institutions. Unless something dramatic happens to focus attention on teaching and teachers, managers spend their time focussed upon resource issues, and not upon teaching and learning. There is no reason to believe that the situation is different in most English schools and colleges. The Fryer Report (1997) on lifelong learning recommended a greater focus on learners and learning and less on management structures and institutions, 'which should be regarded as more or less efficient mechanisms for the delivery of demonstrably high quality learning'. National policy for the professional development of teachers should be complemented by individual school and college policies for the continuing development of all staff.

Teaching is a very complex activity that is affected by, among other things, the subject matter, the time available, the character of the teacher, the dispositions of the learners, resources, and the ethos of the institution. It follows that there is no absolutely right or wrong way to teach, and that teachers need to vary their approach to particular circumstances. Nevertheless, it has been recognised for a long time that there are two general orientations to teaching: a didactic, teacher-centred, skills and drills approach; and a more learner-centred, learning for meaning, constructivist approach.

In practice, one type can masquerade as the other. Supposedly student-centred approaches, for example using group work, can in fact be highly teacher-centred and didactic. Conversely, skilfully presented lectures can give rise to student thought and the construction of knowledge. There is a place for teacher exposition of subject matter, and a place for student assignments that engage learners actively in the construction of knowledge. On the other hand, there are dreary lectures which 'go in one ear and out the other'; and there are poorly conceived and organised assignments that are no more than 'busywork', occupying students' time but teaching little or nothing.

Many teachers desire control – after all, there is usually one teacher and anything up to forty or more students – and both the lecture method and the busywork method give high levels of teacher control. Dictation and teacher-set assignments can both be methods of keeping students too busy to disrupt. To encourage learner autonomy, it is necessary for teachers to exercise control through leadership as distinct from authoritarianism. Teachers have a leadership role in shaping learning for a particular group of learners; this is both an *individual* responsibility to shape a part of the curriculum, and a *collective* responsibility with colleagues to ensure that the curriculum as a whole meets the needs of a particular group of learners. Studies of effective teaching (Tabberer, 1994) have often shown that what is needed is a combination of affect (warmth, respect, and so on) with good organisation. The studies upon which this book is based bear this out.

Listening to learners

If learners and their needs are genuinely to be the central focus of policy and practice, as claimed by policy documents, such as *Learning to Succeed* and school and college mission statements, then it is important to have means to hear their voices, as part of the routine, on-going work of schools and colleges. Learners' views have been notably absent from many debates about change in education, partly because there is a constantly shifting population of students, many of whom in further education are part-time and not well represented locally or nationally. The National Union of Students is mainly focused upon higher education; within some European countries (although not Britain) the voice of school children is represented by the Organising Bureau of European School Student Unions (OBESSU), based in Brussels.

Seventeen-year-old students, having spent many years in education, are experts at recognising the characteristics of 'good' teachers, often expressing delicate balances of characteristics, similar to those found by Klemp and associates in the United States (Klemp *et al.*, 1985). Here are the views of four 17-year-old English students, each of whom was interviewed individually using Q-sort construct elicitation to minimise interviewer bias (Harkin, 1998). In response to the question, *'What do you think your fellow students associate with the term a "good" teacher?'*, these balanced and measured responses are typical:

> Someone who is able to mix a lesson with letting us learn stuff but at the same time not doing so in a patronising way; being able to work with individuals rather than the whole class . . . you've got to respect them but at the same time they've got to respect you; you've got to be able to talk to them not necessarily about the subject but outside the lesson . . .
>
> A level student

> Someone who is always willing to listen to the student's opinion . . . Someone who is also not critical of you if you don't know something . . . he's not trying to put you down when you get something wrong.
>
> GNVQ Advanced Engineering student

> Someone who you can actually learn from . . . and it also comes over not so authoritarian, more as fun . . . not too friendly. Someone who is not so detached from the students.
>
> GNVQ Advanced Business Studies student

> Someone who'll let you be relaxed with, but can make it more enjoyable to learn rather than just standing at the front and writing on the blackboard . . . role plays and presentations, rather than just what they say . . . Treating you as individuals rather than just a class, especially at college.
>
> GNVQ Advanced Health & Social Care student

Discussions of the relationship between teachers and learners with many individual students and groups of students have often touched on their experience of compulsory schooling. Many speak of having felt overlooked by teachers, not recognised as worthwhile individuals in their own right. Many have low self-confidence as learners and look towards years 12 and 13, and further education for a new start.

The Communication Styles Questionnaire (CSQ)

Based on a review of knowledge about emotional growth and learning, Greenhalgh (1994) believes that:

> The ability to meet children's needs is enhanced by the capacity to observe and reflect upon how things are done. Observation and assessment are most useful when they consider the child in relation to other factors which inhibit or promote development and learning: the teacher, the learning environment and the whole-school ethos, the relationship of the child with peers and family, the child's perception of experience.

It is difficult for teachers to observe themselves and observation carried out by other people – colleagues, managers, Ofsted – are usually based on a brief visit, and what is observed may not be the usual pattern of classroom interaction. In order to assist teachers to obtain accurate feedback about how they tend routinely to communicate with learners, researchers at Oxford Brookes University developed a Communication Styles Questionnaire (CSQ) (Harkin *et al.*, 1999) as a valid and reliable instrument that teachers may use *with their students* to evaluate how they tend routinely to interact. It is not intended that the CSQ be used as a means of judging teachers as good, bad or indifferent, but as an aid to self-directed professional development. It provides teachers with a vocabulary to discuss how they tend to interact routinely with learners and a basis to build up a repertoire of communication styles to meet the needs of different learners in various learning situations.

A fuller account of the CSQ is given in Chapter 8. In this chapter, an introduction will be given, followed by insights gained from teachers' use of the CSQ.

The CSQ has two dimensions – *control* and *warmth* – which measure who controls the teaching situation, and the degree of warmth or affectivity in the teaching situation respectively. These two factors, forming a coordinate system, are well grounded in social and clinical psychological research (e.g. Leary, 1957; Argyle, 1982). The model is an holistic one – scales should not be isolated from others and both warmth and control are necessary parts of effective teaching.

Thus one construct or dimension for teaching and learning processes is *control*, which may be divided into sub-constructs, as itemised in Table 5.1.

Table 5.1 Control dimension

Authoritarian	High standards
Prefers students to be quiet and passive, to listen and take notes.	Has high expectations of student effort and performance.
Dominates interaction, even during discussions.	Is fair in assessing against criteria and gives useful, critical feedback.
Uses assessment to control and motivate.	**Instils respect for learning**
Instils fear	
Lenient	**Learner autonomy**
Has low expectations of student effort and performance.	Encourages students to play an active role in learning by, for example, consulting them about activities, setting work that challenges them to find out for themselves and to solve real-life problems.
Is lenient in assessment, passing poor quality work.	
Does not care if students fool around and do not learn.	Encourages student–student, as well as teacher–student interaction.
Instils lack of respect for learning	Uses self and peer assessment to help learners understand what they know and still need to learn.
	Instils responsibility

A second dimension of teacher–learner interaction is *warmth*, measuring the degree of opposition or cooperation in the learning situation. Entwistle (1987), for instance, referring to the work of Bela Kozeki in Hungary, affirmed that, 'there are emotional and moral, as well as cognitive, sources of satisfaction in schooling'. Effective teaching involves not only the shaping of learning but the promotion of a suitable ethos for learning. Language use in post-compulsory education goes far beyond the transmission of information. Importantly, it involves 'warmth', or social bonding between learners, and between teachers and learners. It is in language use and in the patterns of interaction of which language use forms a part, that learning takes place – or fails to occur. The *warmth* dimension may be divided into sub-constructs, as itemised in Table 5.2.

Between them the two dimensions of *control* and *warmth* give rise to eight scales which measure communication style on an orthogonal co-ordinate system. Use of the CSQ in two formats – *Actual* and *Ideal* – completed by a teacher and one or more groups of the teacher's students provides a comprehensive profile of the teacher's and students' perceptions of their normal pattern of interaction. Appendix 1 shows the CSQ (*Actual*) for teachers of learners of 14–19 in schools and colleges; and the CSQ (*Actual*) designed for use by teachers of learners of 19+ in universities.

Figure 5.1 shows a typical set of profiles for a teacher. In addition to the profiles, teachers are also given the scores for the scales and the individual items so that patterns apparent from the profiles may be reflected on in more detail.

Table 5.2 Warmth dimension

Dissatisfied	**Leadership**
Has a basically pessimistic view of students, as people who are unable to act responsibly or to learn successfully.	Designer learning activities with a particular group of students in mind.
Takes little or no interest in students as persons.	Understands the subject and its assessment.
Is heavy-handed in criticism, undermining learner self-confidence.	Is prepared to change tack and vary activities to enhance learning by, for example, drawing on learner experience and interest.
Is prone to sarcasm and/or anger.	
Instils a negative opinion of learner potential	**Instils respect for the teacher**
Uncertainty	**Understanding**
Displays a weak grasp of the learning needs of a particular group of students.	Has a basically optimistic view of students as people who are capable of acting responsibly and of learning successfully.
Appears unsure of the subject and/or the assessment requirements.	Is confident enough to share jokes and humour with students.
Fails to control student behaviour and may abdicate responsibility for this.	Monitors individual performance and gives help when needed.
Instils disrespect for the teacher	Takes an interest in students beyond their role as learners.
	Instils self-respect in learners

Generalisations from using the CSQ

Studies in other countries (Levy *et al.*, 1993; Felouzis, 1994) show that there are differences in patterns of teacher–learner interaction on different types of courses, across different subjects, and often between male and female teachers. This confirms two important facts: firstly, that there is no absolutely right or wrong way to teach; and secondly that different students may require different teaching methods. What these facts give rise to is that many teachers need a *repertoire* of teaching styles upon which they may draw, in response to particular circumstance and need.

The CSQ is intended to give accurate and comprehensive feedback to *individual* teachers, possibly working as part of a team all of whom are using the CSQ. It is not intended to make statements about teachers in *general*. Furthermore, some commentators argue (Silcock, 1993) that 'the assumption that . . . there are skills more likely to guarantee a teacher's success overstretches the responsibilities of the teacher and diminishes the responsibilities of the learner.' Nevertheless, once the CSQ had been used with many different teachers, of different ages, both sexes, across different subjects, institutions and types of

Name	**A teacher**
Institution	**An institution**
Class	**A course**
Date	**A date**

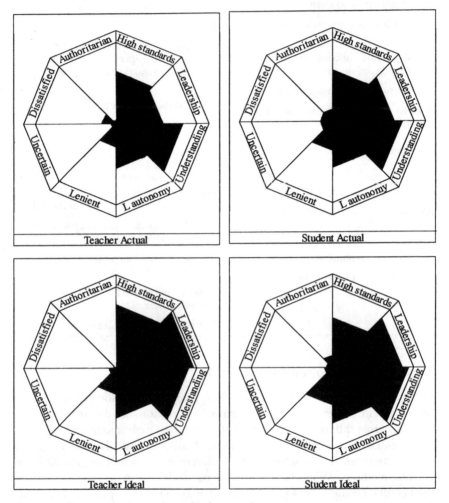

Figure 5.1 Communication style profile for a teacher.

course, it became evident that there may be some general differences that are worth reflecting on.

In general, teachers who have used the CSQ are seen by their students as having a positive profile – demanding reasonably *high standards*, showing good *leadership*, being very *understanding* and allowing moderate *learner autonomy*. This contrasts with low scores for *lenient*, *uncertainty*, *dissatisfaction* and *authoritarian*.

Teachers echo these responses but with a tendency to accentuate their positive qualities. Compared with students' ratings, teachers tend to see themselves setting *higher standards,* displaying better *leadership* qualities, showing greater *understanding* and allowing more *learner autonomy.* Differences in learner and teacher perceptions shows a need to promote teacher–student discussion about communication styles.

Teaching experience

Students' responses show differences in the communication styles of teachers with different levels of experience. Teachers with less experience (under 10 years) are often less strong on leadership and more uncertain and dissatisfied than their more experienced colleagues. Some differences by length of experience can be explained in terms of a developmental process. Brekelmans and Creton (1993) noted that newcomers to teaching often have little experience of leading others and seem to take up to 10 years to develop a style which portrays consistent leadership skills and self-confidence. During this period they seem to allow more student control and appear less warm compared with their more experienced, settled and self-assured colleagues.

Teacher age

Both from the students' and teachers' perceptions, differences in the age of teachers seem to have little direct bearing on styles of interaction.

Differences between courses

Use of the CSQ shows that there are often differences between the patterns of communication in different types of course. Typically, GNVQ courses give rise to warmer, more interactive patterns of communication than A levels. This may be attributable to several factors, including possibly that A level students and teachers may be more focused on the subject than on the quality of the process, whereas GNVQ students may, in general, have had more difficulties previously as learners and, therefore, display a need for more supportive interactions. GNVQ courses may also be designed to encourage more co-operation, through group work assignments and negotiation of learning goals. The downside of this may be that a focus on relationships leads sometimes to tensions between learners, and between learners and teachers, as the nature of the relationship changes.

Students on A level courses tend to experience less control over their own learning than students on GNVQ courses; and A level students feel they attract less lenient attitudes towards the standard of their work than those on GNVQ. Teachers strongly echo these student views.

Students of more technical/mechanical and mathematical subjects perceive that they are given less autonomy over their learning compared to students of other subjects, and teachers corroborate these differences. The subject of learner autonomy will be returned to later in the chapter.

Learning and the importance of affect

Use of the CSQ with teachers and their students has given rise to the important insight that, in the perceptions of both teachers and students, the most important dimension in effective interaction is *warmth*. This is so for students of all levels in post-compulsory education; across academic and vocational areas; and across subjects. 'Warmth' in teaching is a delicate balance of several factors, the most important of which are *leadership* and *understanding*.

Leadership emphasises that teachers must *manage* the processes of learning for the benefit of learners, who should sense that they are in the 'safe' hands of someone who cares about their welfare and their future.

Understanding emphasises the importance of qualities such as *genuineness*: being personally involved in the relationship; *acceptance and trust*: acknowledging that the other person's experience is different to one's own but valid; and *empathy*: figuratively being able to stand in another's shoes (see Rogers, 1961, 1969, 1983). *Understanding* is shown by simple things such as knowing student's names, sharing a joke, taking an interest in students beyond the narrow confines of a subject.

Most teachers score highly on these scales but virtually all teachers and students want even higher scores. Most teachers self-scored on these scales more highly than their students' perceptions; and most teachers had even higher personal ideal perceptions on these scales than their students. In general, if teachers were perceived by their students as the teachers perceived themselves, then all would be well. Human communication, however, is never that straight-forward.

Teachers can improve *leadership* by activities such as improving student perceptions of the organisation of learning by giving them a clear sense of direction through, for example:

- giving a sense of being dependable
- letting them know what will be covered and why
- clarifying and simplifying learning objectives
- explaining the purpose of tasks and assignments
- informing them of the assessment requirements in advance
- reviewing what has been covered
- checking on individual learning and giving specific feedback on how to improve, without 'putting the student down'.

Teachers can improve *understanding* by activities such as:

- knowing students by name and using names other than for admonishment
- sharing a joke
- recognising when individuals have difficulty
- showing patience
- helping students with work
- spending a little time talking to students on topics other than education.

Teachers often face a set of dilemmas (cf. Berlak and Berlak, 1981), such as to make the learner feel secure *and* at the same time to encourage learner autonomy. Effective teaching is a balancing act in which the primary skill is liking for learners.

Liking learners, in this context, is a professional attitude or stance towards learners that needs to be felt by the learner if it is to be effective. It is not the same as being a friend or confidante. It is impossible for teachers to establish friendship with all learners – there are too many of them and they change every year. Liking for learners in a professional sense, is more limited and may be demonstrated by relatively simple acts such as using personal names for more than admonishing; a friendly smile; an encouraging word; a few minutes spent asking how someone feels. These are the small courtesies of everyday interaction and are as important in the classroom as in the rest of life.

Thus, the *affective* domain, represented by teacher behaviours such as recognising individuals, listening to students, showing respect, being friendly, sharing a joke, making some self disclosure, is fundamentally important. This may not be recognised when allocating resources, drawing up staff timetables, training teachers and organising colleges. In England, teachers in further and higher education are expected to teach ever larger student groups, for more hours per week, although for fewer hours per student group, thus making it increasingly difficult for teachers to relate to individual students. An increasing number of staff are part-time, which may make it more difficult to be available to students outside formal lessons. The drop-out rate from English post-compulsory education is high and one reason may be that some students (especially those who are struggling) may have too little sense of being valued as individuals, and of having a supportive, friendly relationship with teachers.

The literature based on compulsory schooling shows a strong link between the quality of teacher–learner relationship and effective learning. Seminal works that touch on this subject have been written by Rogers, Winnicott, Bowlby, Hall and Hall, and Salmon, among others, and were summarised by Greenhalgh in *Emotional Growth and Learning* (Greenhalgh, 1994). This literature shows convincing evidence that improving the quality of human relations in an institution also improves the quality and amount of academic work produced and the attendance of the students. The relationship between the learner and the teacher is central to the learner's experience.

Learners with emotional and behavioural difficulties are particularly in need of teachers who will pass time with them outside formal teaching, acknowledging them as persons and boosting their self-esteem. For all learners, the *process* of education is as or more important than the *subjects* learned.

For post-compulsory education, research on the interaction between teachers and learners by Harkin and others has shown the vital importance of affect or *warmth* in that relationship. A factor analysis of the eight scales of communication interaction showed that the 'warmth' dimension is just under three times as influential as the 'control' dimension (Harkin and Davis, 1996b). This has been corroborated by studies of the constructs that 17-year-old students use informally to evaluate their teachers by Harkin (1998) in England and Johannessen *et al.*

(1997) in Norway. This is so even for engineering students who stress instrumental aspects of learning more than, say, health & social care students.

The importance of affect in education was recognised in *Flexible Learning in Schools*, a report produced for the Training Agency, funded by the Department of Employment (1990):

> Schools which have adapted most happily to the development of Flexible Learning . . . tend to be those where there is:
> a recognition that
> – how students relate to each other
> – how students & staff relate to each other, and
> – how staff relate to other staff
> are importantly interconnected.

The report recognised that 'The quality of the relationship between a teacher and a young person is a vital factor in encouraging learning and growth'. The relationship should be neither 'that fear and contempt which used to stalk school corridors' nor 'the casualness which implies there is no distinction in role between teachers and students'.

Paradoxically, the report *Flexible Colleges*, produced by the Further Education Unit (1991) for the Department of Education, made no mention whatever of this factor. Industry it seems can talk openly about the importance of human relationships, while education – at least in the Thatcher years – had to pretend that it was all about the dispassionate, value-free transmission of information. The enigma of the missing human relationships is deepened by *Flexible Colleges'* opening contention that 'Flexible learning requires students to be active learners. There is an emphasis on the process of learning and the ability to learn, rather than on the acquisition of knowledge; an emphasis on problem-solving, on the ability to interpret situations and to take the initiative'. This is an approach that ought to place human communication at the centre of the analysis.

Developing learner autonomy

The relatively instrumental and pragmatic nature of post-compulsory education, orientated as it is towards adulthood and work, may be assumed to give rise to a transmission model of the curriculum, in which the role of the teacher is to transmit skills, knowledge and understanding to learners, in an ethos in which affectivity is minimal. The results of our research show this to be far from the case. Both learners and teachers wish the ethos of learning to be purposeful but at the same time to possess a 'human face', in which learners are treated as responsible partners in the learning process, although it should be remembered that the concept of 'ethos' or 'climate' is one that may vary greatly from learner to learner. Nonetheless, mutually respectful working relationships are at the heart of successful education, as they are of most human endeavours.

Teachers have a legitimate authority in any learning situation. They are paid

to take responsibility and to manage learning in the interests of learners. Their subject expertise and experience, together with their pedagogical knowledge and skills, enable them to help learners achieve mutually agreed goals. Teacher control can, however, be exerted in two broadly different ways: through *leadership* behaviours and the setting of *high standards*, or through *authoritarian* behaviours that limit the possibility of developing learner autonomy.

The thrust of new initiatives in further and higher education is that learners should take more responsibility for their own learning. This arises for a mixture of ideological, pedagogical and pragmatic reasons: ideologically, it may be desirable to empower learners; pedagogically, more active participation by learners in the learning process may result in longer-term and deeper learning; pragmatically, the recruitment of more learners with less per capita resource means that it may not be possible to teach and learn in traditional ways.

An important insight from using the CSQ with teachers and their students is that about 50 per cent of teachers and students wish for more *learner autonomy*. The concept of autonomy is vague – the Greek roots of the word, *autos*, self and *nomos*, law indicate a set of human characteristics such as personal knowledge, awareness and responsibility. For most students, this is focused upon things such as having some choice about what topics they study and how they are assessed, while teachers take a broader view that incorporates students taking more responsibility for finding things out for themselves. Wilde and Hardaker (1997) summarised the implications for teachers as reducing lectures (shown by Bloom, 1956 to be ineffective in encouraging deep learning) and using a wider repertoire of teaching strategies, providing good quality resources for independent learning, negotiating learning goals, self and peer assessment, and activities such as teamwork and presentation. The rhetoric of providing students with a new start as learners is strong in further education. It is often claimed that young learners will be treated as adults. The reality, however, is sometimes different and patterns of teacher–learner interaction may be similar to those found in secondary education. In particular, teachers may be uncertain about whether to treat young people as adults in the hope that they will respond; or whether to wait until they behave as adults before treating them as adults. Of course, the term 'adult' here is being used as code for displaying behaviours such as self-control, listening and responding appropriately, being polite, concentrating and focusing on the work in hand. In general, it is more effective to treat young people as 'adult' and most will respond appropriately, most of the time. Even adults do not always behave in 'adult' ways; and even teachers can have 'off' days. Once a suitable learning climate has been created, then there is room for manoeuvre, to make allowances and not let relatively trivial issues get blown out of proportion.

Some students are very restricted in the opportunities they have for developing and controlling their own learning. This may be particularly problematic for students of engineering and mathematics, and may also be problematic for some A level students. If all students are to be enabled to be more responsible for their own learning, as recommended by the Dearing Report (1996), then some teachers will have to develop a wider range of interpersonal behaviours to encourage this. There is a need to promote reflection and discussion by teachers about communication styles in order to identify, try out and adopt alternatives that will raise levels of student autonomy when appropriate.

If it is thought desirable to give learners more responsibility for their own learning, then teachers need to learn how to share their power. *Control* behaviours (which are not altogether inappropriate) need to be tempered with other behaviours. For some teachers, a fundamental shift is needed which will not be easy, from teacher-dominated to teacher-sharing lessons. This shift would be accompanied by significant changes in language (towards more adult–adult exchanges); affectivity (towards more use of personal names, and acknowledgement of feelings).

Teacher 'control', as we have seen, may be displayed in relatively positive and relatively negative ways. Positively, it is possible to establish and maintain control by setting *high standards*. Negatively, it is possible to attempt to control learner behaviour through being *authoritarian*. The latter puts a lot of teacher energy into maintaining the dominance of the teacher in determining what may be said and done, by whom, when, for how long, and so forth. If learners object, as many do and in many different ways, then the teacher may have to expend more and more energy in trying to maintain control. The setting of high standards, by contrast, places the locus of control beyond a battle between teacher and learner in the quality of work to be accomplished and the effort to be expended. Teachers model high standards by behaviour such as returning work promptly, marking fairly against open criteria, giving useful feedback, attending lessons punctually and being well-prepared.

High standards merge in one direction with *authoritarianism* and sometimes it is necessary for teachers to be authoritarian and, for example, not to tolerate bullying or racism. In the other direction, high standards merge with *leadership*, which gives learners a sense of being in the safe hands of someone who understands the subject and its assessment and cares about learner success.

In summary, learners reach Year 10 and beyond with a vast experience of education but often with very few mechanisms and opportunities to discuss and address the impact of changing perceptions of need, new learning goals, and the processes of learning and teaching. They are generally expected to get on with the business of learning in an unquestioning way, not always with the most appropriate results. This need not be the case. As we shall see further in chapter seven, by providing teachers and learners with a common vocabulary with which to reflect on and discuss their experiences of education, the Communication Styles Questionnaire (CSQ) can be a starting point for mutually beneficial development of learning. The demands upon teachers may then be faced by them more in partnership with young adult learners who, as active participants in their own education, may be helped and encouraged and given the skills necessary to take growing responsibility for their own learning. Chapter 6 will show how teachers may use a variety of strategies to encourage more active engagement by learners.

Part III

Putting learning theories into practice

6 Making learning more active

The purposes of this chapter are threefold:

1   To reinforce the principles outlined in previous chapters, which show that learning is enhanced when it is social, active and experiential.
2   To add practical examples to the theories outlined in Chapters 3 and 4 which lay down the underlying principles upon which the best learner-centred approaches are built.
3   To demonstrate to teachers how to encourage learners to feel comfortable with their own learning style and that they can operate effectively across all styles.

We hope that teachers of all subjects will feel encouraged to customise these techniques to their own situation, though the subject origins of each idea are stated.

Facilitating learning through experience: examples of Dale's Cone in action

One of the main benefits of Dale's Cone (1946) is as a planning tool for teachers who wish to use student experience as the starting point for either one lesson or for a sequence of lessons. The first two examples are included to illustrate the potential of the Cone in academic teaching.

Sociology

In studying family life, the teacher of A level Sociology could suggest numerous approaches. For example, students could observe and analyse their own family, visit neighbours or a family in another country; they could watch a TV programme such as *The Simpsons*, or read sociological articles on the family. Quite often the preferred approach is through academic texts and government statistics.

Dale's Cone (Figure 6.1) allows the teacher to help place the various options in some sort of relationship to each other within a framework. The lower down the

Figure 6.1 Dale's Cone in Sociology A level.

Cone, the more immediate is the experience on several levels: physical, emotional, subjective, cumulative. The higher up the Cone the more detached, objective and comparative. A case can be made for taking any route through these choices. Indeed there are many variables within the concept of family (single parent structures, divorced parents, various types of extended families and so on) which would influence one's choice of starting point and route – and why the teacher might choose to 'shuttle' between the various experiences.

General Studies or Philosophy

One of the topics in an A Level General Studies programme was 'Values and Beliefs'. The only information available to the teacher was a selection of past examination papers and copies of the Chief Examiner's reports. The teacher felt that the topic might be too personal for 16-year-olds to talk about or one where they might affect indifference so it would need careful planning to make it interesting and relevant. The teacher used a mind map (Figure 6.2) to explore possible resources and to sketch out early thoughts about a coherent scheme of work. The mind map was then translated into Dale's Cone, as shown in Figure 6.3.

Many ready-to-hand resources could be drawn upon, such as *Sophie's World* (Gaardner, 1995); encyclopedia entries for items such as the US Declaration of Independence and the 1689 Bill of Rights; visual material from Sunday newspaper supplements and from the Internet; a video recorded programme on 'Ayers Rock'; and artifacts such as photographs and religious exhibits. The first lesson would start with 'direct purposeful experience'.

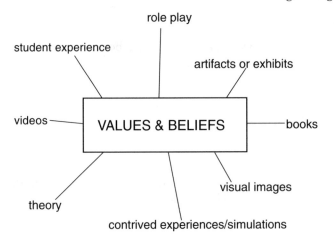

Figure 6.2 Values and beliefs mind map.

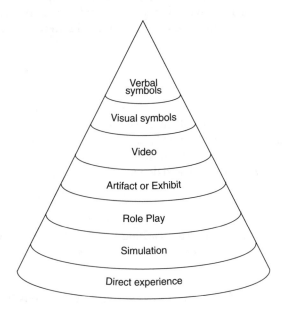

Figure 6.3 Values and beliefs using part of Dale's Cone.

Lesson One: belief as a matter of individual principle

The lesson proceeded as follows:

PHASE 1 INDIVIDUALS

The students were asked to think of something they would never do as a matter of principle and write it on a card.

PHASE 2   PAIRS

The students swapped cards with a partner and then they had to think of three circumstances where their partner's principle could be tested.

PHASE 3   PAIRS

The pairs then tested each other's principle.

PHASE 4   WHOLE CLASS

Each set of principles was discussed by the whole class. The teacher introduced the need for agreed publicly accessible statements of principle.

PHASE 5   TEACHER

The teacher passed round the Bill of Rights 1689 and a starred excerpt from the US Declaration of Independence. Principles, circumstances and exceptions were addressed. The students learned of the role of the 'premise' in presenting an argument.

Lesson outcome

It worked well enough. There were all the usual icebreaking problems of a new lesson, a new teacher and a new group and all that, so it could only be classed as a qualified success. But it signalled two important features to the group of the way the course would be taught: (i) the lessons would make full use of student experience; and (ii) the style would be open and democratic.

Leisure & Tourism

Dale's Cone is also a valuable planning tool for teaching vocational subjects. The following example, taken from GNVQ Leisure & Tourism, is on the topic of *Consumers and Customers*:

- Verbal symbols: legal issues (Trades Description Act, Sale of Goods Act, etc.);
- Visual symbols: various pie charts and other graphic representations of statistics;
- Video;
- Artifacts/exhibits: actual promotional material;
- Study trips/visits: trade fairs, departmental stores, big events, public buildings, tourist attractions;
- Dramatised experience: role play in the form of a group presentation;
- Contrived experience: a 'project' on promoting something, like a sandwich or a new line in chocolate;

- Direct experience: as students are both consumers and customers real materials such as chocolate or sandwiches can be used.

The value of Dale's Cone to the teacher of young adults

The value of the Cone can be seen through a number of dimensions.

- It expands our notion of the concept of 'experience', thus making more explicit the choice of possible teaching approaches in the first phase of the experiential learning cycle. The teacher can either harness direct experience where it exists or introduce new experiences through iconic or symbolic activities. Confirming the validity of personal experience makes it easier for learners to reflect on their current perceptions and for the teacher to challenge them with new theories.
- The enactive phases of the Cone engage learners in a variety of ways which are socially interactive. Role play, simulation, use of pairs and groups and so on require learners to share ideas and to test out their experience with other learners.
- Learner autonomy is enhanced. The teacher transmits an unspoken message that learner perceptions are central to the learning process and not peripheral; that the teacher's role is as enabler or facilitator.

Facilitating learning through information processing: the Taba model in action

One of the main benefits of the Taba model, also known as the Integrative Model (Eggen and Kauchak, 1988) is its ability to capture student experience through the use of 'data retrieval charts'. The concept of a data retrieval chart is simple; it is another way of looking at the *rectangle*. The rectangle dominates information processing in the modern world. Its place in most classrooms is often physical, with the chalkboard or the whiteboard being the most fixed point. The rectangle can almost hypnotise the teacher into teacher-led activity and can paradoxically sometimes stifle communication because students often feel conditioned into recording what is on the rectangle to the exclusion of thinking and discussion.

Types of rectangle in use in education and training

- The traditional blackboard
- The whiteboard
- The flip chart
- The wall chart
- The book
- The A4 handout
- The computer screen
- The television screen.

Ideas which need to be shared or made known must be 'captured' in such a way as to make them accessible. Most teachers have been using the essential data retrieval or organising framework of the Taba model for many years without necessarily being aware of it. Within the 'rectangle', teachers use various pictorial or visual formats to capture ideas. Common visual devices include: columns, tables, charts, maps, sketches. Any visual 'model' can be used to represent reality for a student's experience. Figure 6.4 is a reminder of the Taba model.

The following examples will give a flavour of possible variations

Retail

In a 'classic' Taba style lesson, students were asked to list things they would find in a supermarket. After the usual grouping and labelling phases the teacher then organised the class into four groups, assigned them all a different supermarket to visit and asked them to write the location of each category (fruit, dairy produce, detergents, etc.) on their data retrieval chart.

The students went to the various supermarkets, completed their assignment, and presented their findings to the whole class in the next lesson. The student 'models' were then used for comparison, generalisations, explanations and predictions in classic Taba style. An example of one completed student chart is given in Figure 6.5.

1	2	3		4	5	6	7
list	group	categorise	data retrieval chart	generalise	compare	explain	predict

Figure 6.4 The Taba model.

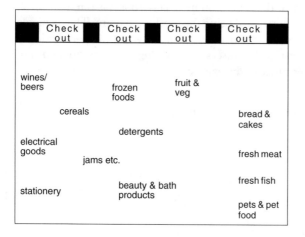

Figure 6.5 Completed student data retrieval chart.

When each group had presented its findings the teacher facilitated a discussion about the reasons for the differences and similarities and provided additional teacher input in the form of a handout. The engagement of the students was enhanced by the process of being actively involved in collecting the data. The theory which the teacher introduced was made more intelligible to the learners because it built on their visual and practical experience.

Motor vehicle

Another example of a data retrieval chart comes from a motor vehicle class. The students were asked by the teacher to brainstorm what comes into mind when they think of the fuel system of the car. The answers they gave were things like: carburettor, petrol tank, petrol pump, pipelines, fuel injection nodes, etc. The teacher collected their ideas and then asked the students in pairs to use the 'model' in Figure 6.6 to insert where they found each of the items applying to the vehicle which they had been allocated. As in the Retail example, the students returned to the whole class on completion of the task and their findings were presented and compared. The teacher used their experience to establish some of the basic design principles in modern car fuel systems (Figure 6.6).

Charts in plan form are effective as starting points for capturing learner experience in a variety of subjects:

The layout of a wood machine workshop

The students were asked to list the range of machines found in a machine shop and then to write on the plan provided the optimum position of each to the others for efficiency and Health and Safety. Again the lesson was followed by discussion and teacher input on Taba lines.

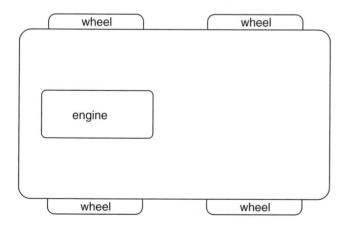

Figure 6.6 Student data retrieval chart for motor vehicle class.

Play activities

The students on an 'early years' course were asked to list the range of activities they had seen on their placements in various playgroups and, using the plan provided by the teacher, decide the best place for each activity, taking into account the numbers of adults and children and any Health and Safety implications.

A restaurant situation

The students were asked to work out the possible seating arrangements for thirty guests at a function, having been given the plan of a room and its tables. Then, after further instructions from the teacher, they had to decide the best way to organise the room for a particular function. Once again the teacher used the student presentations for comparisons, generalisations, explanations and predictions in classic Taba mode.

Veterinary nurses

This is an example of a matrix, such as that in Figure 6.7, where the teacher supplies data and the student has to tick the appropriate box. The same principle can be used in most subjects: simply change the categories in the data section.

The use of Taba is particularly useful in academic subjects such as A level Sociology, Economic Geography or Politics. A common academic approach is to start a Taba sequence with a completed data retrieval chart and then begin the student–teacher interaction at phase 4. Eggen and colleagues (1979) use the bar chart shown in Figure 6.8 to demonstrate how the teacher of Economic Geography or Politics could begin a teaching sequence at phase 4. The teacher

	weight	temp	blood	foetus	feeding
data > Words and/or pictures of a mare in foal to six months					
normal					
Abnormal					
• monitor only					
• needs treatment					

Figure 6.7 An example of a matrix.

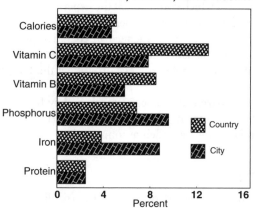

Figure 6.8 Taba interaction starting at phase 4. From Eggen *et al.*, *Strategies for Teachers: Information Processing Models in the Classroom.* Copyright © 1979 by Allyn & Bacon. Reprinted/adapted by permission.

can help students process the information contained in the chart by asking the following series of questions which follow the sequence of phases four, five, six and seven in the Taba model:

- *Phase four*: What is the biggest dietary deficiency among rural families? What is the biggest dietary deficiency among urban families?
- *Phase five*: How would you compare rural and urban families with respect to vitamins and minerals? How do rural and urban families compare overall?
- *Phase six*: Why do you think rural families have fewer problems with phosphorus deficiency than do urban families? Why do you think rural families have greater problems with vitamin C deficiency than do urban families?
- *Phase seven*: If federal money were spent to alleviate problems in the area of dietary deficiency, what type of programme would alleviate both urban and rural problems most effectively?

Eggen and colleagues (1979) endorse this approach as follows: 'this sequence is designed first to familiarise students with the data in the chart. It then asks them to generalise about the information in the graph and finally to explain and apply the information they process.'

The value of Taba to the teacher of young adults

- It provides another way for the teacher to use the experiential learning cycle. Dale concentrated on opportunities for varying experience, whereas Taba concentrated on the 'cognitive processing' of experience. The three stages of data, organising framework and inference impel the learner to engage with new ideas and theories in ways which complement the experience, reflection and abstract conceptualisation phases of the experiential learning cycle.

- The accent on the learner being actively engaged in cognitive processing encourages social interaction. It is data collected and discussed by students which provides the means for the teacher to develop student thinking skills in drawing inferences.

- If this process is made transparent to the learners, then they become less passive in the techniques of structuring knowledge. They learn to 'scaffold' inferences themselves and thus increase their autonomy.

Facilitating active learning

The principles of active learning are not dedicated to a particular author or 'model', therefore, the following examples are described by type of activity:

Posters

The following example is used to illustrate a fundamental point. A History teacher in a comprehensive school had the task of getting his GCSE students to detect bias in newspaper accounts of the events of 'Bloody Sunday' in Londonderry, Northern Ireland in 1972. He distributed a selection of accounts from seven different newspapers of those events to the class. The results were disappointing in that only three out of twenty-five students could detect any sort of bias at all. The task is quite sophisticated but the results were still disappointing. Of course there may well have been a number of reasons for the low achievement in addition to the difficulty of the task: the ability of the students, the task may have been too demanding at that age for the average student, the task may have been poorly presented, and so on. But the teacher felt it would be damaging to class morale as well as a reduction in the percentage of marks the students might achieve through their course work if the issue were left unresolved.

Having reflected on the problem in Kolb terms, the teacher came to the conclusion that the approach to the task had been too analytical and that most students needed guiding round the experiential learning cycle. In the next lesson, they were divided at random into groups of five or six, given photocopied images from books, magazines and newspapers, flipchart pens, scissors and glue sticks and flipchart paper and required to produce a propaganda poster on behalf of one and only one of the protagonist groups in Northern Ireland. The actual choice of protagonist group, the Social Democratic and Labour Party (SDLP), the Democratic Unionist Party (DUP), the Irish Republican Army (IRA) or the British Government was again by random selection. To make the poster the students could cut out and use any of the photocopied images, and they were allowed no more than eight words of their own.

The outcome was well worthwhile. Not only did the posters bring out unexpected reservoirs of creative talent in students who had been mostly non-contributing members of the class but the groups used identical material for opposite reasons. What a gift for the teacher who was able to demonstrate from the students' own work the possibility that the same data could be used for diametrically opposite purposes. When the class returned to the original newspaper articles, there was a dramatic improvement in the ability of almost all the students to detect bias. They had been guided by a judicious use of the experiential learning cycle. The lesson was active in the terms described in Chapter 4 because the students had experienced bias, by *creating* their own propaganda, before being asked to *react* to bias in the viewpoint of others.

Other examples of active learning

A poster example can take a whole lesson but teachers often feel they would like to have some shorter exercises or activities, lasting 5 or 10 minutes, which are essentially active. Since 20–30 minutes' listening is the limit for most people even when they are fresh, they wish to minimise the amount of passive learning in the lesson. Here are a number of options which qualify for the epithet *active*:

Assertion–reason

This is an example from A level Politics to illustrate the way that an assertion–reason approach is constructed. The assertion and the reason are both written as complete sentences which make sense in their own right. There may, or may not, be a connection between them but a connection is implied. It is the students' job to decide whether the statements themselves are true or false and whether they are linked as implied.

Assertion
William Hague is the best leader the Conservative Party has ever had
Reason
His policies on Europe have been the most carefully thought out

The learners are invited to tick two boxes of a grid, as shown in Figure 6.9, to show whether or not they agree with the assertion and the reason. The benefits to the learners come from the discussions and the way they defend their views.

Assertion–reason examples are active in the terms described in Chapter 4 because the students have to *solve* something, i.e. they have to make a decision based on reasoned argument.

	right	wrong
assertion		
reason		

Figure 6.9 An assertion–reason grid.

Elimination

A teacher introduced a group of NVQ level 2 Catering trainees to a theory lesson as follows:

> Here are six possible ingredients for this dish. What would be the effect if I forgot to include ingredient 'x' (then 'y', then 'z')? In pairs decide what the effect would be. You will be expected to justify your answer.

Another example can be seen in a class of NVQ level 2 builders. The teacher says: 'Here is a job card. There are fifteen tools which you might think are needed for the job but you are only allowed to choose ten. In pairs decide which would you choose and why'. This exercise need not apply only to builders; for example, nurses have used the same technique in teaching what is required on the resuscitation trolley.

A further example concerns a teacher of GNVQ Intermediate Leisure and Tourism who wanted a class of students to think about the requirements for Association of British Travel Agents (ABTA) registration. He devised a checklist which included all the correct requirements plus two maverick items which should not be there – the learners were asked to eliminate the mavericks.

Elimination examples are active in the terms described in Chapter 4 because, instead of students copying what teachers have written on overhead transparencies or white boards, which is a passive task, the students are required to process information *actively*.

Backward chaining

Backward chaining was developed first for students with profound learning difficulties where the teacher completes the whole of a task such as feeding and encourages the student to complete the last stage. Then the last two stages, then the last three and so on.

A variation on this technique is where the teacher presents the learners with the correct answer first and then introduces a series of versions which differ by one variable. The students are asked to find the difference and to say what the effect might be. The example in Figure 6.10a, b and c of the water cistern, taken from Belbin *et al.* (1981) is a good illustration. The correct diagram and two incorrect ones are included here but in the original there are eight incorrect ones.

An example of backward chaining

This technique has been adapted by different teachers, each one asking the same questions: 'What is wrong? and What would the effect be?':

* A teacher of secretarial skills gave the learners a perfect letter and then four or five examples which differ by one or two variables.

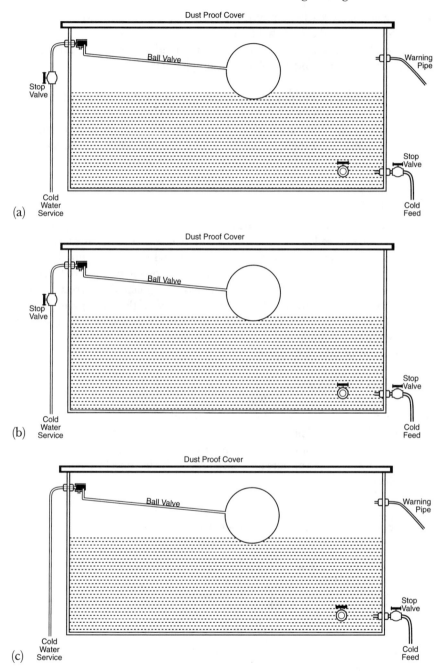

Figure 6.10 a, b, c. An example of a backward chaining activity. From Belbin *et al.*
(1981) *How Do I Learn?*, Cambridge: Further Education Unit.
Crown copyright is reproduced with the permission of the Comptroller of
Her Majesty's Stationery Office.

- An electronics teacher showed the class a perfect circuit and a number of versions where there was a difference.
- A teacher of early years education presented an approved layout of a playgroup setting and a number of examples of changes.

Forward chaining is also possible. Chaining, backward and forward, is active because it is process driven. Learners are supplied with first principles and then encouraged to use observation, deduction, and group support to show how far they have internalised these principles. Quite complex ideas can be taught to students in this way rather than by passive initiation by the teacher.

Matching

The principle is straightforward: the teacher creates two sets of categories. One set of categories is called, say 1–8, and a complementing set is called, say A–H. The learner is invited to make a series of eight matching pairs. Figure 6.11 is an example from a theory session in catering. The following two sets of categories are wrongly matched and the students are asked to make the correct pairings. The learners correctly matched the items of food with the appropriate form of preserving enabling the teacher to open a discussion on the connection between food storage and usage.

Here are some other examples:

- textures and effects with techniques or tools (GCSE Art);
- years with events (GCSE History);
- symptoms with illnesses (HND Veterinary nurses);
- oils with associated powers (Aromatherapy);
- x number of job cards and y number of possible processes – which card would be most appropriate for which process? (Electrical Installation, Motor Vehicle).

Form of preserving	Item of food
1. canning	A. chips
2. 'kilner' jar bottling	B. cereals
3. freezing	C. olive oil
4. vacuum sealing	D. rocket salad
5. packet	E. peaches in brandy
6. silver foil	F. baked beans
7. conventional bottle	G. sugar
8. 'plastic' sealed bag	H. chocolate

Figure 6.11 An example of 'matching' from catering studies.

Matching is active because it compels learners to process information and make decisions.

Sorting

Sorting is a simple technique which most learners love. The teacher devises a number of 'cards' which are put into envelopes. The cards can be of words, pictures, artifacts or any combination. The instruction is then given to sort them into two or more piles. There are innumerable instructions for '*sorting*', such as:

Legal	Illegal	(A level Law)
Mandatory	Voluntary	(Electrical Installation)
Political factors	Social factors	(History)
Loose compound	Stable compound	(Chemistry)
Pre-World War 2 houses	Post-World War 2 houses	(GNVQ Construction)
Ferrous metals	Non-ferrous metals	(GCSE Physics)

It is possible to devise activities with three, four or more ways of sorting. Sorting is tactile, even with cards with just words on them. Learners can make changes and alterations as they process their thoughts. Sorting can be social if done in pairs (often the best approach) or threes. It is active because the learners are able to rehearse possible misconceptions or anxieties and know that the teacher will help them to reconcile them.

Ranking or sequencing

Ranking has features similar to sorting and eliminating. Cards or artifacts or lists are used to set up the ranking. Sometimes the same effect can be achieved by brainstorming. Ranking works well when a priority is required:

- The best sequence for a planning application (Town Planning);
- The progress of protein through the digestive system (Biology);
- The safety sequence for a particular application (Electrical Installation);
- The correct process for connecting an electrical circuit (Physics).

One refinement is diamond ranking where a teacher gives out nine cards, say, on the factors influencing customer satisfaction and asks the students to diamond rank 1–2–3–2–1, as in Figure 6.12.

Games

There are many books on educational games. Good examples are found in Brandes and Phillips (1979) and in Bowkett (1997). Teachers can also adapt games found on TV or available commercially for their teaching. Examples include:

Figure 6.12 A diamond ranking.

- *Trivial Pursuit* in languages. The teacher adapts the commercial game by devising questions and answers in the target language.
- *Connect Four* on the whiteboard. The students have to make a correct sentence from a menu of possibilities and each 'correct' response gets a naught or a cross following the usual *Connect Four* rules.
- *Alibi* (again in languages). The teacher sets a scenario, for example a robbery, and the class is divided into pairs to concoct a shared, plausible alibi for their whereabouts at the time of the incident (hence the name). Then one member of a pair is sent out and his/her partner is questioned. The partner is then brought back in and questioned to see how well their stories tally. The teacher and the rest of the class have to judge which is the likely robber.
- *Pen portraits* (again in languages) The teacher writes on different cards the name of a famous person, alive or dead, real or fictitious; or a famous place, such as Buckingham Palace; or a historical object; or whatever is preferred. One student fetches a card from the pile and can answer only 'yes' or 'no' as other students try to guess what is on the card.

Games are useful to teachers of both academic and vocational subjects in that the learners see that learning can be fun and that the teacher has made the effort to identify with their experience.

Texts

In most academic subjects there is often a large amount of factual information to disseminate. It is always useful to be able to vary the way text-based material is presented. Quite often teachers wish learners to immediately read a passage of text in the form of a handout but past experience has shown that most of them do not concentrate on the task. There are several ways a teacher could counter this tendency:

- Extract one or two key learning points or elements from the handout and say to the students: 'I have taken out two key ideas from this article. See if you can tell me what they are'.
- Use a handout where there are gaps in the text and ask the students to supply the missing word.
- Cut out the sub-chapter titles from a handout and write them in a jumbled

form on the board or a separate piece of paper. Ask the students to match the appropriate sub-title with the appropriate section.

- Cut up an article or handout into sensible but random chunks, give out some glue sticks and get the learners to correctly re-assemble it.
- There are lots of possibilities for getting individuals, pairs, groups or any combination of these to pick out what they think are the 'keywords' or the most significant arguments in an article, newspaper extract or similar. Put some sort of limit on this activity, e.g. ask students to pick out *five* keywords or the *two* arguments which . . ..

Rehearsal

Many learners are too embarrassed to make contributions off the top of their head in a question and answer session, often because they are afraid to be thought stupid or they just haven't thought of anything appropriate in the millisecond allowed to respond. In well-motivated and well-ordered classes they are often deemed to be quiet but in less well-disposed classes they can appear to be sullen and uncooperative. Activities which allow learners to interact with ideas and concepts and *rehearse* their views with other students before being exposed to a more open, whole class session can often change the whole class-room climate.

One could argue that '*rehearsal*' is a theme common to many of the short exercise ideas which have been looked at in this chapter. Sorting, matching and ranking are all forms of rehearsal in that they encourage learners to actively engage in processing ideas before they have to formalise the learning, but there are several other rehearsal approaches such as:

- Giving learners a self-rating instrument like the ones which are often used to determine individual learning styles.
- Using examples from each learner's own experience ('Can you think of a person in your own life who was a good leader? What were the x number of essential qualities which made you think she/he was a good leader?'). Working in groups, the learners then make a list which they use to relate to theory presented by the teacher.
- Asking learners to handle or observe real life artifacts. A typical instruction might be: 'You have 5 minutes to look at this: What do you think it might have been used for? Which country might it have come from? You should be able to point to some evidence for your decision'.

The value of facilitating active learning to the teacher of young adults

There are many benefits in facilitating active learning approaches.

- Such approaches allow the teacher to start some learning sequences in the fourth, active experiment, quadrant of the experiential learning cycle.

Moving round the cycle in a clockwise direction, each activity adds to the learner's experience and the feedback transforms the learner's sense of *ownership*. For many learners the whole process assists the acquisition of theory.

- Rehearsal is a form of reflection in action, but whereas reflection in the Kolb sense involves the *direct* engagement of learners with their own experience, rehearsal is more *indirect*, achieved through the process of being active. The effect on the brain is to subconsciously compel it to accommodate to new phenomena.

- In most of the examples in this chapter, active learning subsumes a social dimension. When learners examine their existing ideas and deal with the challenges of alternative viewpoints they are operating in a social context. The teacher does not have to occupy the central position in the classroom for the whole lesson, thereby acting as the pivotal point which channels all ideas. The source of energy for the learning comes from the learners and not solely from the teacher .

- Being actively engaged in processing ideas through any of the active learning methods included in this chapter makes learners more autonomous. Learner ideas and experiences are seen to have high status which ultimately fosters self-reliance. Learners taken through an active learning process are better equipped to deal with an environment which is increasingly information driven than those whose experience of learning is largely controlled by the teacher's agenda.

Facilitating learning through problem solving and problem-based learning

Problem solving does not have a universally accepted academic definition or model and the term can mean different things to different people. The model chosen here is based on the idea that in every problem there is at least one *objective* and at least one *obstacle*. The problem is solved when the objective is achieved and the obstacle overcome.

For analytic purposes, there are distinct stages of problem solving.

- *Identification and interpretation.* What sort of problem is it? Can I/we solve it? Have we seen something similar before?
- *Decision making.* What might be done? Who should do what? How long have we got? What resources do we have?
- *Implementation.*
- *Evaluation.*

Types of problem

For our purposes, there are probably three types of problem.

'Real' problems

These occur when learners are doing real-life tasks in a real situation. Trainee caterers in training restaurants satisfying the needs of customers; trainee hairdressers cutting or styling the hair of customers; learners in the workplace. Most NVQ assignments are real problems since they are assessed in the workplace or near equivalent.

'Training' problems

Almost any lesson can be turned into a mini problem-solving session by thinking of a process *verb* such as sort, rank, match, locate, select and so on.

Problem-based learning

Gibbs (1992) explains the concept:

> problem-based learning involves learning through tackling relevant problems. This is distinct from learning how to solve problems (problem solving). In problem-based learning the problem may not be solvable but nevertheless provides a rich environment for learning. The aim is to learn rather than to solve the problem.

There are many well-known versions of problem-based learning such as: simulation, business games, case studies and the application of theoretical 'modelling'.

Designing problem-based lessons

Broadly speaking there are two styles of problem-based learning: a '*closed*' problem where there is one preferred solution and an '*open*' problem where there may be a number of plausible solutions.

'Closed' problem-based lessons

COMPLETING A SPECIFIC SET OF INSTRUCTIONS

An example of this type of problem is the 'indivisible load' exercise where the students working in groups have to solve a logical thinking problem in the shortest possible time. The problem is expressed in an identical instruction to the leader of each group as follows:

> You are the manager of a Transport Department. You have been informed that a large vehicle has to get from the works to the dock gates. The other members of your team hold different pieces of information which will help

you plan the whole manoeuvre. Your brief is to draw out from the other members all the information necessary to solve this problem.

The groups are then given a map with a number of obstacles: the width and height of bridges; time taken to go round roundabouts, round right-angled corners and across level crossings; angles which the vehicle can and cannot negotiate; and half-mile markers on all roads. Each member of the group has different items of information which will help solve the problem, e.g. the fact that it is illegal for such a load to travel outside the hours of daylight, and that there is a specified time by which the vehicle must arrive at the dock gates; and details of trailers which go at different speeds and can carry different weights.

ORGANISING WORK LOADS IN NVQ LEVEL 2 HOTEL AND CATERING

The students were asked to divide a sheet of paper into three columns labelled: *daily cleaning, weekly/monthly* and *occasional.* On a separate sheet of paper they were supplied with a list of tasks and their 'problem' was to decide the appropriate column for each task, such as:

- take any lost property to the housekeeper or supervisor;
- replenish towels, soap, etc.;
- change shower curtain;
- wash carpet or reseal floor if necessary;
- give a special clean round all taps and plugholes;
- clean bidet and toilet.

BROKEN INFORMATION

This idea appears in *Problem Solving at Work* by Bruce Burgess (1983, 1986). Groups are given a story or situation which contains a problem. The task is to arrive at the correct solution to the problem. To make the exercises work successfully the teacher should devise:

- A story or situation which is as realistic as possible.
- A problem arising from it.
- Enough information to solve the problem plus several 'red herrings'.
- About three times as many pieces of information as there are members of the group. Each piece of information presented separately on card, kept in an envelope or wallet. It is advisable to write on the envelope the total number of cards and make sure the students count them all before commencing the activity.

Figure 6.13 is an example, based on Construction, of the top copy of all the information needed to solve a problem, including distracters. Each box

* The problem is that there is a damp patch on the bathroom wall	The answer (obviously kept from the students till the task is completed): **damp has crossed the cavity due to mortar on the wall tie**
The problem occurred half way up the wall at 1.2 metres	The down pipe had come away from the guttering
Damp on both the inside and outside wall	Cavity wall construction had a 50mm gap
The bathroom was well vented	The house was built in 1990
The wall construction is held by wall ties	House bricks are porous
Engineering bricks are impervious	Mortar is mixed at a ratio of 5:1
Fairy liquid was used as a plasticiser	'Febmix' is a plasticiser
Hand made bricks are more irregular	It had been raining a lot - 2cm in 36 hours
There was no window in the bathroom	The house was built without any cavity insulation
A plastic damp proof course (DPC) was used	Browning was used to plaster the bathroom
The bathroom incorporated a shower	There were four teenage children living in the house
The house had had several owners	The inside walls had been painted with emulsion
The outside bin was built using hand made bricks	Breeze blocks were used for the inside skin
Cavity walls should always be kept clean	

Figure 6.13 A broken information example.

represents a card (twenty-six plus the answer card) which the teacher cuts up and puts in an envelope.

'Open' problem-based lessons

Many open style problem-based exercises contain characteristics seen in the *closed* ones: a map or fixed physical parameters, information given to different members of the group for the 'leader' to coordinate, constraints of time or space or speed or size and so on. The chief difference is that open questions are influenced by assumptions which affect group decisions.

'GYMKHANA' EXERCISE

This exercise was designed for small groups and the leader given a brief, 'You are the person responsible for organising the car parking arrangements at the local gymkhana. You call a meeting of volunteer marshals to plan the parking. The team is all the personnel you will have on the day. What you need to do today is:

1   find out what the other marshals know and can do;
2   decide approximately how many vehicles the field will hold;
3   decide what will be the best use of the team on the day;
4   decide how the traffic will flow.

A map of the field shown in Figure 6.14 is given to the group and each marshal is given a different amount of information to contribute to the decisions. Each marshal knows information that will need to be shared. For example, marshal 1 knows that there will be twenty-four competitors in the gymkhana and that their vehicles must be accommodated in the field; marshal 2 can obtain lots of equipment such as: ropes, posts, loud hailers, sign making material, coloured tape and so on; marshal 3 knows that four coach loads of supporters will be arriving on the morning of the gymkhana; marshal 4 owns the field. He knows that there is an area approximately 15 metres × 15 metres, which gets boggy after rain.

The teacher can vary the amount of information depending on the purpose of the lesson. If the most important outcomes are application of number, or organising an event, then it may be better to let the students obtain accurate dimensions of vehicles; whereas if the exercise is really about group work and communication then the teacher may not be too worried about accuracy.

All the groups will come up with different solutions because they will all make different assumptions: whether to use two gates or one, whether the traffic should flow anti-clockwise or clockwise, where to put the coaches, whether the trees could be used to provide shelter for horses, the style of car parking and so

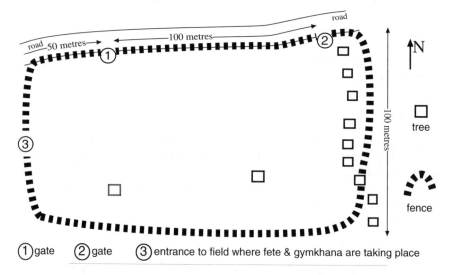

Figure 6.14 The map for the car parking at the gymkhana.

on. Among the considerations which teams will confront are Health and Safety for visitors, competitors and animals, access for disabled visitors and competitors, needs for those whose transport is on two wheels, space for coaches and trailers to back and turn and so on.

Other examples of 'open' problem based learning

MOTOR VEHICLE: WORKSHOP WORKLOAD

The teacher gives these instructions:

> You are the boss of a small country garage. You have two mechanics working for you and do not do any mechanical work yourself. You need to organise the jobs for tomorrow for two mechanics so that everything gets done between 08.00 and 17.00.

> Mechanic 1 has worked for you for 6 years and is fully qualified. He is the only one qualified to undertake MOT tests. Mechanic 2 has been with you for 1 year and is fully qualified. The two mechanics both start work at 08.00, they stop at 10.00 for a 15-minute break, then work till 12.30 when they have 1 hour for lunch. After lunch they work till 15.45, have a 10-minute tea break and finish work at 17.00.

> The workshop has one four-post ramp for MOTs and for other repairs when there is no MOT work. There is one two-post ramp. There is room for a third car in the workshop but this does block access to the two ramps. Some jobs can normally be done outside but the weather forecast is for rain all day. The parts company with which you deal guarantee to deliver within the hour.

> Below are the jobs and all the relevant information. *On the two sheets provided show how you would plan the jobs through the day for the two mechanics and where the jobs will be done*:

> Six MOT tests. Each MOT test takes 45 minutes. All the MOT cars will be there by 07.30 and will not be collected till 18.00.

> Ford Escort saloon 1989 1.3 cc for a new clutch. This model was built in a year when clutches were changed and there is a possibility of four different clutches, so until the gearbox is removed you will not know which clutch to order. Normally the complete job would take four and a half hours and can only be done on the two-post ramp. The car is being dropped off at 10.00 and must be ready for collection by 16.00.

> Rover Metro 1988 1.0 cc. In for a new radiator which has already been

delivered. The car will be dropped off at 08.00 and you have promised it at 09.00 for collection. The job takes 30 minutes and does not require a ramp if the bottom hose clip is facing upwards.

And so on – descriptions are given of several other vehicles, allowing the teacher to make the task more or less complicated. The students are given a timetable (Figure 6.15) for each mechanic.

HAIRDRESSING

A good example of the use of 'open' problem based learning is the hairdressing teacher who had only two sinks in the training salon. This had caused many problems and a deal of friction in the class so she devised a problem-based activity to sort out the problem.

She set out a number of customer requirements which included a perm on hair never before permed, a renewed perm, a colour change, a cut and blow dry, a re-dying of 'blonde' hair and so on. Some of these needed the sink and some did not. She divided the students into groups and asked them three questions.

- How would you arrange the appointments for the best use of the two sinks?
- What resources need to be replaced in the store?
- What times would you telephone the taxi to pick up customers a, b, and c?

The students were faced with a problem which concerned them but which had no ideal solution. They had to come to a conclusion which was both workable and acceptable.

The teacher's role in problem-based learning

Whichever type of problem is chosen, the teacher's role is crucial. In the real problem it is the teacher, trainer or supervisor who decides with the learner that

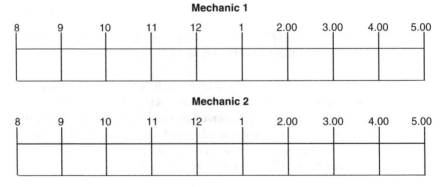

Figure 6.15 Workshop work organiser.

the problem is within their capabilities and acts as a resource, support, or safety net. The teacher has usually ensured that the learner understands the theory and has the practical skills to cope and is ready to proceed. In the problem-based version it is the teacher again who ensures that the learner has the necessary skill, experience and knowledge to benefit from the exercise. In the training version, the appeal of using this approach for the teacher is that it utilises the natural learning style of pragmatists and activists. A problem-based lesson provides an experience for the students to reflect on which gives an immediate illustrative edge to any lesson.

Problem solving strategies are of value to the teacher for a number of reasons:

- They increase learner motivation through a major change of arousal.
- Though they often begin with action or experience, well designed problem-solving lessons embrace all elements of the experiential learning cycle thus encompassing all learning styles. This is especially true of broken information activities where, in the reflection or debrief stage, the teacher can talk through student ideas, queries and misconceptions; and where the whole process can be used to consolidate theory.
- They make full use of the social dimension of learning. The design of the problem compels learners to work in teams and to develop key skills.
- In common with other facilitative approaches, learners can be 'trained' to be more proficient in the process of learning and to be more confident in their own skill and those of their peers. Problems challenge the learner and they help reduce their dependency on teachers.

Learning through deduction and cues

In Chapter 4 it was asserted that learners know far more than some teachers will allow. This 'knowledge' may not be manifested in terms of fact or erudition but can be found in their ability to use observation, visual cues, signs, gestures and their thinking skills to respond to new situations. An example of this was noted by a teacher in charge of students on a work experience exchange to Munich. Some of the party were studying A level German but others only had a rudimentary grasp of the language. The whole party was expected to make its way from the airport to a prearranged rendezvous with the host teacher and students which involved finding the correct underground railway platform. The A level German students and the teacher looked at the information boards and attempted to find the information they needed through their skill in reading German. But the three non-A level students began to run off in a certain direction exhorting the rest of the party to follow, which they did, though with bad grace. When the teacher caught up with them he asked why he should believe that these three knew the direction when much more competent German speakers were still trying to work it all out. 'Easy' they said, 'all the U and S bahn lines are colour coded. Ours is coloured red and is S6'.

This is not a unique phenomenon. Learning which is structured to utilise student skill in deduction and association can be very effective. Four examples follow:

A science lesson called 'What's in the box?'

A teacher collected about a dozen small boxes or packages, placed one or more items in each (dried peas in A, milk bottle tops in B, a ping-pong ball in C, and so on) and then sealed them. The students were placed in groups and asked to work out what items they thought each box contained.

After all the groups had attempted to identify the contents of all twelve boxes, the teacher gave a few cues: 'Is there one object, two, or many? Does it roll? Is it hard or soft, heavy or light? What is the sound – is it metallic?' The students were given more time to identify the contents and in the debrief they shared their solutions and their strategies.

Early education and the 'feely' bag

A bag is filled with a variety of items of different size, shape and texture to encourage sensory exploration. The students cannot 'see' the objects, only 'feel' them. They have to try to deduce what each object could be and to compare their theories.

Masked photographs in A level or GNVQ Photography

This idea is adapted from one published in Bowkett (1997). In an A level photography class students are given different versions of the same picture, each with a different section masked off, and asked to imagine what the 'missing' section might be to encourage them to learn about form, composition and impact.

'Computer friendly'

This is an exercise which a teacher can give to a group of learners who are on an introduction to word processing course, perhaps in the first or second lesson. The idea is to let them discover some of the effects which a computer can achieve by deduction and observation. The students are given the following instructions:

Read this poem, called version A and then identify the differences in version B.

Version A

I can do many things with my computer
Make my work look smarter and cuter
When I get up to speed
I won't even need
This course or even my tutor

Version B

I can do **many** things with my <u>computer</u>

1.   Make my *work* look   cuter

When I ₉ₑₜ up to `speed`
When I get **up** to speed

●   I won't even need
    This course or even my tootur

                                              smarter and

When the students have completed the comparison of the two versions, the teacher gives out the 'answer' sheet below.

List of icon-led functions for the 'poem'

The poem was originally typed in Times New Roman script, font size 14 and with a left-side margin. I have made **15** changes which were:

*   Two changes of font size (a 10 and an 18)
*   one change of script (Courier)
*   one word made bold
*   one word in italic
*   one word underlined
*   one line indented using the indent icon
*   one line with a bullet point
*   one line which begins with a number
*   one picture inserted into the text
*   one (only one, I hope!) spelling error
*   one line centred
*   one line with a right margin
*   one line copied
*   two words cut out and pasted somewhere else.

Your next tasks are as follows:

1   Using the handout of the Microsoft Word toolbar at the top of your computer screen, see if you can work out which 'tool' you would use for each effect in the above list.
2   Type out the original poem and then see if you can make the changes yourself. Remember to use the mouse to highlight the part or parts you wish to change before you use the appropriate tool. If you go wrong, the *Undo* tool

will take you back to the point immediately before the change you have just attempted.

The value of learning through cues and deduction to the teacher of young adults

Learning through cues and deduction contains many of the benefits of all the other facilitative approaches discussed in this chapter; the positive use of all learning styles, the social dimension of learning, the increase in learner autonomy and the increase in arousal.

In addition there are some particular benefits from the selective use of this approach:

- learning to think on one's feet, to cope with restrictions on knowledge and to deal with some elements of uncertainty or approximation;
- learning to apply the whole range of one's knowledge and learning in an unfamiliar setting;
- learning to combine sensory clues with imagination when judging the nature of data and the inferences one might draw from it.

These qualities are hugely important in preparing students for the unexpected in public examinations, in job interviews and for the world of work.

Facilitating learning using current technology

The digital camera

Use of technology can transform the teacher's options in theory sessions in even the most standard classroom. This example involves the digital camera. Most teachers find theory lessons more challenging than practicals, especially at certain times of the day or week. If teachers can be self disciplined so as to use a digital camera to record practical work when it is in progress, then the possibilities of customising meaningful theoretical exercises to which the students will relate is much increased.

The teacher takes digital photographs of the class in a practical situation. These are used in a later 'theory' lesson. Adopting an approach which is similar to the Taba model, where lower order questions precede higher order ones, the teacher can ask simple questions such as: 'What was happening here? What tools are being used? What safety issues have been addressed?' More complex questions will follow such as: 'Look at this series of photos and tell me if the sequence of operations is correct' or 'You all used this piece of equipment last month – explain in your own words how it works and the principle(s) on which it is based'.

A variation on using photographs can be achieved if the teacher also downloads relevant information from the Internet and incorporates photocopyable materials from catalogues or magazines into a task sheet or assignment brief.

The use of students' own experience creates an 'active' dimension to the theory. The mutual reinforcement of each part makes the learning more enjoyable and more powerful, especially when the students can help in the production of the theory exercises.

Use of floppy disks

In this example the teacher makes a 'master' disk on which information is placed, some of which is accurate and some of which is misleading or false. Each student is given a copy of the floppy master disk and asked to edit the information. The choice of topics is endless and the method can be adapted by any subject teacher. The teacher can then either collect the disks and assess them without the students being present or get the student(s) to explain how the changes were identified and what they have learned.

The value of learning through the use of new technology to the teacher of young adults

The benefits are similar to those found in the other facilitative approaches discussed in this chapter: the positive use of all learning styles, the social dimension of learning, an increase in learner autonomy and an increase in arousal. Moreover, young adults relate well to new technology: they identify with it socially and in their personal life and its educational value is part of their experience.

Conclusion

Teachers teach in different ways and have their individual styles. Some prefer formal settings with a high degree of teacher direction, especially in the first half of a lesson. Others favour a facilitator approach with a high degree of student involvement. There are all sorts of variations in between. Many teachers are able to change or modify their style, depending on the subject being taught. Because teaching is such a personal endeavour, the examples included in this chapter may not be of immediate appeal or inspire the reader to try a particular strategy. This is to be expected. There may be a host of factors which affect the choice of strategy. What we have attempted to illustrate through the examples here are a variety of techniques which utilise all aspects of student learning styles, make learning active where possible and increase motivation to learn. The emphasis has been on process, facilitation and inclusiveness because the evidence in Chapters 3 to 5 has shown that this is where a change in teaching behaviour is most needed.

If a teacher wishes to adopt a more facilitative teaching style, there are four questions to address in each lesson plan:

1   How much of the lesson is directly dependent on the teacher for information and pace?

2   What are the students expected to be doing in each phase of the lesson?
3   Is this lesson basically similar to the majority of my lessons?
4   Are any learning styles or types of intelligence being over emphasised?

In the first question the issue is one of *dependency*. There are short-term and long-term dangers in the teacher doing too much of the work. In the short term, notably in the actual lesson, this approach relies either on the teacher or the intrinsic worth of the subject matter to inspire student interest. But if the teacher feels below par or the topic is dry, teaching becomes hard work and students can become restless. In the long term, the problem is potentially more dangerous. Students who are over taught as young adults can experience difficulties when faced with a greater emphasis on self directed learning, notably in Higher Education or at work. They may lack the key skills needed to cope when teacher assistance is less intimate or immediate.

In the second question the issues concern teacher–student *relationships*. Teachers who are committed to active learning project a sense of trust and openness to their students. They are process oriented and see the movement from the particular to the general as being the strategy most likely to produce effective learners. In this regard the Taba system is a valuable addition to the planning skills of the teacher.

The third question mainly addresses *motivation*. The over use of any stimulus in any aspect of life can lead to a down turn in performance and involvement. The value of many of the activities included in this chapter lies in their novelty to the students and not in their familiarity, a phenomenon first noticed in the Hawthorne effect. They are reinforcers that can lift the energy levels of the students at the right strategic moment. Even the occasional change in strategy, from mainly passive and teacher directed to more active and student focussed will increase student interest and willingness to learn.

In the fourth question the issue is one of *inclusiveness*. A check on provisional timings will often resolve any problems. If the dominant activity of the majority of lessons is of learners being expected to acquire information passively, then this should ring warning bells to the teacher. Students with activist or pragmatist learning styles will feel excluded. Their exclusion may not manifest itself through disruptive behaviour but it will emerge in low enthusiasm and performance. A revision of Dale's Cone may well rectify the issue.

Changing one's teaching style from high teacher control of content, pace, structure and expected outcomes to one which values a more student-centred ethos needs practice. The students may not immediately show that they have enjoyed the change in style but perseverance will pay dividends.

7   Developing awareness of styles of teaching

When it comes to self-awareness, teachers may be expected to be as blind-sighted and as far sighted as any other human beings. They may be prescient and sensitive to some of their personal characteristics and myopic about others. Use of the Communication Styles Questionnaire (CSQ) has shown repeatedly that a teacher's self-perceptions of how they tend to teach are often different to the perceptions that students have of them (*see* Chapter 5, Figure 5.1). There is nothing surprising or necessarily worrying about this. What should concern teachers, as professional communicators, is that they be aware of the likelihood that this is the case for their own individual practice; and should also be aware of their own preferred styles of teaching. Unless their professional development is based upon this knowledge, how can they progress? How can they ensure that they are actively engaging learners and facilitating learning through social interaction (Chapter 3)? How can they decide how best to motivate, challenge and actively involve their students in learning (Chapter 4)? How can they recognise which strategies will be most appropriate for their particular subject and students (Chapter 6)?

In teacher training much is made of the concept of *reflective practice*. Drawing upon the work of Kolb (1984) and the experiential learning cycle, and the work of Schön (1983, 1987) it is taken almost as axiomatic that teachers should reflect on their experience, draw measured conclusions from this process, and plan new practice on the basis of these conclusions. If teachers wish to reflect on their preferred or habitual teaching styles, they would normally go about this reflective process by introspection, mulling over their teaching, thinking of what seemed to work and what didn't work so well. They might draw on the views of colleagues, and they may even draw on 'hard' evidence, such as the views of learners or assessment results.

What the CSQ offers is more detailed and comprehensive feedback based both on a teacher's intrapersonal perceptions of how they tend to teach with a particular group of learners; and also upon the learners' perceptions as they respond to the same questions. A teacher and a group of students each complete the Questionnaire in two formats: *Actual* and *Ideal*. The *Actual* format elicits the teacher's and the students' perceptions of the interaction that occurs routinely; the *Ideal* format elicits the respondents' perceptions of how they would prefer to interact. The results from the use of the CSQ may then be reflected on by the teacher to see if there are areas that she or he wishes to target for development.

The next chapter will give a more detailed description of the CSQ. In this chapter, several examples will be given of teachers who have used the CSQ in order to develop their teaching. The examples show how the CSQ may be used to reflect on and develop professional awareness of how you tend to teach; and how some teachers have gone beyond this to attempt to actually change aspects of their teaching.

The teacher trainer

Whilst a student herself undergoing teacher training, her expectation had been to see really expert teachers in action as role models to give her ideas. Now having taught for some twenty-two years and passionately involved in training others, her hope was that she was an exemplar to her students, having no problem with the thought that they may expect her to be really good. But was she living up to her own ideals, modelling what she considered to be best practice? And what were her students' views of her teaching and their real expectations?

She undertook a review of her teaching. The CSQ was completed by her and two parallel groups of students from the same Certificate in Education (Further Education) course. This resulted in two sets of profiles identifying 'actual' and 'ideal' behaviours, as perceived by the teacher and students. Follow-up discussions were held with the student groups on the basis of the CSQ data.

Both sets of profiles were excellent. The trainer felt she was setting consistently high standards, providing good leadership, offering a high degree of understanding and learner autonomy – perceptions which were clearly echoed by her students. As far as the ideals were concerned, both she and the students felt there was room for some improvement. However, this meant almost perfection in some scales, underlining the view that those undergoing teacher training place high demands on their trainers.

On the face of it, the profiles suggested that the trainer's communication style provided a warm, supportive environment in which students had freedom to direct their own learning. But some of the finer detail of the feedback raised some interesting differences between the perceptions of the two classes and also between those of the trainer and her students. One group saw her as being slightly less strong in leadership, understanding and learner autonomy and more dissatisfied and authoritarian than the other group. They displayed generally differing needs from the other in terms of their ideal – in addition to the common desire for more choice in assignments and greater awareness when they did not understand, they wanted from their trainer more help with their work, more opportunities to present work to their peers, less sarcasm and less apparent dissatisfaction with them.

Reflection on this information and the subsequent views and comments from the discussions led the trainer to focus on two issues. How was it that she believed she was treating the groups in the same way but this was not perceived as the case by the students? And is it ever appropriate to use sarcasm in teaching?

Her thoughts prior to reviewing her communication style were that she treated the two classes in the same manner – they were on the same course, at the same stage, getting the material in a slightly different order, but with her seeing them frequently and having the same expectations from both. Often she got the groups muddled up and when marking a piece of work could not tell which group the student belonged to until she looked it up. So she began to explore the make-up of the two classes to see what might account for the differences in perceptions. General ability levels were much the same but the group which rated her less highly consisted of students with more problems, personality conflicts between some of the students and more sporadic attendance by the students. Talking through her reflections, she became aware that maybe the students' perceptions of her were affected by their perceptions of each other – those receiving a lot of attention because of difficulties or personal problems could be seen by others in the group as being the cause of them receiving less attention. The challenge then for her was this – if this is the case, is there really a need or way for her attention to be better balanced between the students?

The question concerning the use of sarcasm exercised her greatly. Although her personal belief was that sarcasm should not be used in teaching because of the detrimental effect it often has on students, it was in fact her natural style and sometimes 'slipped out'. The mature students in these two groups had varying views on the matter. On the positive side it was considered as paying someone attention, treating them as adults, offering them a learning opportunity as to whether or not to respond, a form of humour or emotional release; on the negative side its use was seen as humiliating, controlling and hurtful, with the consequence that some students drop out of the educational system. Aware that conflicting views prevail on this matter, even within herself, her reflection is leading her to consider this – as a teacher trainer, should she use sarcasm herself and how should she deal with it when observing and assessing other people teach?

The nursery nurse teacher

Eight years ago she became a teacher, motivated by a combination of interest in the subject, enjoyment in helping people to learn and the thought that it would be a career move. Four years ago she completed her training and acquired a Certificate in Education. The kind of relationship she was trying to build with her young students was one which engendered trust, built confidence and provided encouragement so they could be more proactive and independent in their work. However, she admitted that since finishing her Certificate in Education she had got out of the habit of reflecting on her teaching, something which appeared to be exacerbated by few opportunities to talk with colleagues or staff developers about the teaching process, because of time constraints. Hoping to get some new ideas about how to teach, she participated in the Communication Styles project and reflected on her teaching with four groups of students over a twelve month period. Feedback from the CSQ was supplemented with information from video recordings and subsequent discussions of three teaching sessions.

All four sets of communication styles profiles were broadly similar. For each class the teacher felt that her standards were reasonably high and that a good level of understanding existed between her and her students but that the leadership she provided and the learner autonomy she allowed were only modest. The students' views of the interaction were slightly more critical. As far as the ideals were concerned, both the teacher and the students wanted a somewhat different pattern from that actually being displayed. The desired improvements centred mainly around the dimension of warmth as defined by leadership and understanding. Prominent were issues relating to guiding the students' learning (being more organised, explaining more clearly) and being more approachable (being someone students could depend on, having trust in the students, allowing students to talk to her about things other than work). In some respects these issues were reinforced by the feedback from the video sessions.

Interpreting and coming to some sort of understanding about the feedback from the Questionnaires was something this teacher found quite difficult. Did the differences perceived between her own and the students responses exist in reality or were they purely a feature of the Questionnaire design? In arriving at their responses how were the students interpreting some of the questions? Was what the students said they would like really the most appropriate thing for them? Was the kind of ideal communication style she indicated as being desirable something she really felt comfortable with? As she mused on these questions, she gradually focused her reflections on two aspects: her own interpretation of leadership and her belief in the importance of the teacher–student relationship.

The term 'leadership' was not something she felt very comfortable with, attributing to it characteristics such as dominance and authority. Instead she preferred to use the word 'signposting', believing that it more appropriately conjured up her style of directing and guiding her students towards a specific outcome in their learning. Initially she felt what was being advocated by the CSQ was 'leadership' in an authoritarian, rather than 'signposting' sense. But as she unpacked her own understanding of 'leadership', several of the underlying characteristics which emerged were those highlighted in the Questionnaire feedback, in particular relating to organisation and clarity of explanations. Thinking about what she had done that year, she realised that being pressed for time she no longer provided students with a weekly programme of what she was going to teach and tended to have several, sometimes conflicting, objectives in a session in order to cover everything. She recalled two things from past experience: that students had expressed how helpful it was to have the structure of the course laid out for them, and that when she simplified her aims more was achieved than when she piled things on. She resolved to address these issues accordingly, feeling that the nature of the students – young adults, lacking self confidence and appropriate life experiences for the course – really warranted a more organised approach to help them feel more secure and to see that at least she, as the teacher, knew where she was going.

The Communication Styles model struck a chord with her in respect of the importance of the quality of the teacher–student relationship. Although convinced of this, she faced something of a dilemma in trying to reconcile time constraints, course requirements and aspects of professional conduct with creating a higher level of understanding. She felt because she was only part-time that this contributed considerably to students perceiving her as unavailable and not dependable; she thought the structure of the course itself, always ticking boxes and assessing people, bled warmth out of the relationship because they were working to performance criteria all the time; and she considered that to a certain extent she had to model to the students the kind of professional relationship they would be expected to build up with the parents of the children they cared for. However, having been reminded that her relationship with the students is central to their learning, she became aware that she had no expectations of the students caring for her as a person, instead thinking all they wanted was to have a decent teacher. Reflecting on this, she has begun to open up to the students and share more of herself than usual in an effort to build warmer relationships.

By reintroducing a process of reflection into her teaching this teacher did not acquire the new strategies she originally hoped would be forthcoming. Instead she was reawakened to certain practices and beliefs that she held to be important but had let slip or forgotten since completing her training. As a result her reflections focused on ways of teaching and relating that, despite constraints outside her control, would reassert her values.

The teacher of communication

In his early to mid-50s, he has been a teacher for eleven years becoming fully trained in 1992. He works in the Health and Social Care and Supported Education department of a Further Education college, mostly on GNVQ Intermediate courses teaching modules in communication and interpersonal relationships. He is very committed to caring for his students – the objective of most of whom is to obtain a job in some sort of care situation but he recognises that many frequently arrive on courses needing care and support themselves, having low academic achievement, a sense of failure, and emotional and behavioural difficulties. Therefore, in his care and support of the students, he sees his purpose as a teacher being that of a role model to the students in respect of what they will be employed for. He viewed his participation in the Communication Styles project as a means to further his professional development and over a period of 12 months he completed the CSQ with four groups of students. A discussion based on the feedback from the Questionnaire was held with one of the groups to substantiate and expand the results.

The student profiles from all four groups were very positive about his actual communication style. They perceived him as having moderately high standards and allowing reasonable learner autonomy with good levels of leadership and understanding. Their ideals desired no change with regard to standards but an increase in respect of leadership, understanding and learner autonomy. His own views shared some similarities with those of his students. Like them he thought he had reasonably high standards and good understanding but unlike them he felt he allowed slightly less autonomy and provided very poor leadership. His ideal indicated a desire to increase his standards, levels of leadership and understanding but with no change in learner autonomy. His reflection on the CSQ feedback centred on his perceptions of his leadership abilities and tensions surrounding students directing their own learning.

He explained that by nature he is very self critical and felt that his low estimation of his leadership qualities was not due to any lack of confidence but more to do with the attitude 'I must always do better'. He had to acknowledge, however, that his students believed he did a better job than he thought and in reality what he provided by way of leadership was not far off the students' ideal. Reflecting on the inescapable fact that every group held the same opinion he began to alter his self perception. He realised that he had underestimated himself and, consequently, he revised his opinion of how he was doing, giving a boost to his confidence in the process.

With regard to learner autonomy he felt somewhat in a quandary. He believed that many of his students were unable to direct their own learning being in a state where they needed support themselves for personal problems before being able to apply themselves or concentrate on their college work. Even when he considered increasing their autonomy he found it difficult to see how this could be achieved without him becoming more controlling. In any event he felt constrained by the nature of the GNVQ and structure of the subject and admitted a need to balance any increase in learner autonomy against getting the students through the course where freedom of choice could be a hindrance. His response to learner autonomy was altered to a degree following the discussion held with one of the student groups and a consequent piece of action taken by a colleague.

The students had intimated when completing the CSQ that they would like more autonomy, particularly with regard to the choice of the assignments they completed. The discussion revealed that their definition of choice was actually very limited, referring not to a number of alternative topics for assignments but rather to the opportunity to choose an assignment which matched their learning style, which in this instance was predominantly visual. A second teacher teaching this same class acted on the students' suggestion and arranged for their next assignment to be visually orientated and set by the students, with some considerable success. Seeing that the students' view of learner autonomy was extremely restricted and that they responded well to being given more autonomy within their own realm of ability and expectation, he became more disposed towards the students taking greater ownership of their own learning. This is evident in two ways. One, he is considering offering students on future courses the opportunity to design their own assignment, within the guidelines and pre-set conditions of the course. Two, he has built a time of mutual reflection into his tutorial times with his students, where together he and they consider how each are doing in the teaching and learning process.

For this teacher, using the CSQ and holding subsequent discussions with his students has helped his teaching practice to evolve by enabling him to think about what he was doing. Consequently, he has been encouraged to view himself in a more positive light with regard to his leadership skills and to see learner autonomy as a diverse construct which can be tailored to the desires and capabilities of the students in question.

The teacher of undergraduate accounting

According to this teacher:

> Much learning in accounting is traditionally associated with relatively narrow focus learning outcomes. This is necessarily so, given that graduate profiles include familiarity with the kinds of skills that are essential in professional practice. Students come to perceive accounting learning as acquiring practical skills, through practice from experienced practitioners: learning the right way to manipulate and present the figures. Lecturers, too, can fall into a belief that accounting education largely comprises this kind of activity. In some ways, it is also easier to plan a lecture around explanation, demonstration and worked examples ... While accepting that such skills are important, it is also entirely possible that an accounting education based entirely on these can ignore the importance of learner autonomy in developing the potential of students to learn for themselves.

This particular lecturer's experience whilst teaching on modules designed by others was one of dissatisfaction with the pre-set conditions which he felt constrained the way he provided for students' learning. In his opinion, workbook exercises and rote learning limited students' opportunities for guiding and developing their own learning. He believed that things could be done differently and set out to incorporate this in a new module he was preparing. Before finalising the module he compared his students' views with his own by completing the CSQ. Were his perceptions of the teaching and learning process accurate and would his students welcome any change?

Reflecting on the feedback from the CSQ confirmed his view. He and the students perceived the current experience to offer very limited learner autonomy and both sets of participants wanted to see this element increased. From the students' perspective they particularly wanted more choice in what they studied and the opportunity to choose the assignments they worked on. With this in mind, he planned and ran the new module expressly to stimulate learner autonomy, develop initiative in learning, and use this to motivate students to better results. Features included:

- encouraging students to use their initiative through contributing suggestions for alternative or additional syllabus content;
- giving students greater control over their learning experience through allowing each student to set their own topic and essay title for the assessed coursework;

- encouraging students to use each other as resources and potential sources of guidance rather than relying solely on the lecturer;
- ensuring that students carried out research for class sessions on which class discussions were subsequently held.

The lecturer monitored and reflected on the impact of the module on his students' experience as it progressed and after it had finished. The CSQ was re-administered to show that learner autonomy had indeed increased and that he was moving towards his ideal. He reviewed and changed his expectations during the course as students discussed concerns with him and fed back problems and requests. He held an end of module discussion with the students which showed that, from their perspective, the new approach was worthwhile but problematic – researching in their own way and time seemed to 'stick more in your head'; however, the newness and openness of the structure, coupled with insufficient resources and a larger than expected class, led to feelings of insecurity and hindered group discussions and student–student interaction. Lastly, he perceived problems of his own with a lack of experience in both teaching the subject matter and in use of the new teaching strategies. However, in respect of the academic outcome, out of a class of twenty, there was only one referral.

Using his reflections on his own and the students' experiences, he refined the module, aiming to incorporate learner autonomy in a way that would not leave the students feeling adrift with a new approach. The syllabus content was reduced to create more time for student-centred activities; the breadth and openness of the assignment was decreased to provide a choice within three categories; he devoted more time to introducing the various teaching strategies, their goals and necessary knowledge and skills; requested more library resources and provided recommended internet resources. As a result of the changes, the outcomes from the assignment improved and so did student–student interaction since the narrower range of syllabus and assignments enabled a greater degree of commonality across what was being studied, engendering a more shared student experience.

This lecturer continues to strive for an emphasis on learners taking more responsibility for and directing their own learning in the modules he teaches. Constraints exist – a module may last only 10 weeks; students rarely know each other prior to taking the module; relationships barely develop to any great extent during these short modules; lack of resources limits opportunities – but he has become aware that despite limitations learner autonomy can be increased. The key to such achievement is to plan opportunities into a module from the start and to build on them over time.

The teacher of Health and Social Care

According to this teacher:

> During my year on the PGCE course I took part in two, on-going, Action Research projects; one, the Preferred Learning Styles research . . . based on

brain based learning and the second . . . the Communication Styles of
teachers research project . . . Both these projects have had a dramatic effect
on my teaching and thinking and have consolidated years of muddled
intuitive thinking and feeling into a justifiable structured and systematic
approach to teaching and learning.

In 1994 I first came across the work of Howard Gardner and his, still
controversial, theories of Multiple Intelligences. I was very excited to find
that there was evidence to support my long held opinion that IQ testing did
not take into account the many other intelligences that human beings seem
to possess, however excited I felt at this time I could not see how I could use
or apply this 'new knowledge' to my own life or my teaching. The brain
based learning questionnaire or self assessment test . . . based on the research
of, among others, Howard Gardner, gave me a tool or vehicle for finding out
more about my learners and their preferred ways of learning and working.
The Communication Styles project, developed by Dr Harkin, gave me a
way to assess the effectiveness and appropriateness of my own communication style with students with mixed abilities and mixed learning styles.

Over an 18-month period this teacher was to discover a way of combining
insights into her own communication style with insights into her students'
preferred learning styles, leading to a specific decision and action to increase
learner autonomy.

The Communication Styles feedback from three of her GNVQ Intermediate
Health and Social Care student groups were broadly similar, with both teacher
and students perceiving good levels of high standards, leadership and understanding and a modest amount of learner autonomy. Although some moderate
increases in leadership and understanding would have been welcomed, it was
learner autonomy which this teacher decided to extend.

A class discussion was held with one of the student groups to find out what
they really understood by having the freedom to learn (as defined by Carl
Rogers) and what they wanted in respect of learner autonomy. The students'
comments indicated they had a relatively narrow view focusing on flexibility in
time-tabling of the subject, accessibility to IT facilities, comprehending the
requirements of assignments and the matching of assignments to student
learning styles or intelligences. The first two issues were perceived by the teacher
as being beyond her control but the latter two were definitely matters she
considered within her sphere of influence. The students elaborated that in order
for them to understand what was involved in the writing up of assignments they
wanted to go through the requirements in greater detail, in class, changing the
wordings where necessary to aid comprehension. The teacher had already
ascertained that the majority of the students had a preference for a visual learning
style. The solution arrived at was to arrange for the students to write their own
assignment, based on the topic and criteria pre-set by the awarding body, using a
film as the main medium through which the students studied, researched, created

and drew together their individual learning. In this way it was hoped that the students would take ownership of their own learning, enhance their understanding of what was required and enable them to complete the assignment in a way that made sense to them.

Both the students and the teacher evaluated the process. The students said they had found it a good thing to do and were enthused by it. The teacher felt that the students had understood the language and assignment better for having written it themselves. In addition, the process seemed to have had an empowering effect which, by allowing the students to find a way into the task, enabled them to take responsibility for their own learning.

For the teacher, this experience has encouraged her to build more opportunities into her courses for the students' voices to be heard and responded to as part of the syllabus. She feels that time spent finding out things like their preferred learning styles, what they have not understood and where there is room for improvement in the way she, as a teacher, communicates with them is worthwhile. The students seem to receive a boost from this, perceiving themselves as being valuable and being provided with more suitable strategies with which to deal with the world. The bottom line for her is that keeping channels of clear communication open with her students ensures both the success of learners and teachers: 'There's very little point in having a bagful of facts, information that you need to pass on, without having a relationship with those learners and without those learners trusting you, and respecting you and without that being mutual. You can't get those things across unless there's a corridor to go through'.

The Sociology teacher

As one of his assignments for his Certificate in Further Education, this teacher reviewed his interaction with three student groups taking either GCSE or A level Sociology. In each situation, the feedback from the CSQ showed positive profiles of his 'actual' communication style. His own and his students' perceptions were fairly close together although he had a tendency to underrate himself, especially on *leadership*. The 'ideal' profiles indicated a desire from all parties for an increase in *leadership* and *understanding*, and a decrease in the already lowly rated *Dissatisfied*. Reflecting on these responses to the Questionnaire, he explained that his wide range of responsibilities within the college had created feelings of frustration and being stretched, leaving little time to do the job to his satisfaction, particularly with regard to lesson preparation and having time for the students. Consequently, he considered that he was having to coast along as best he could. However, he did want to pick up on where things were either working or not working within the interaction taking place in the classroom, wishing through this process to become as good a tutor as he could be.

During the subsequent discussion of the results with each class, it became apparent that the students held him in high regard, confirming the CSQ results that he was approachable, friendly and able to talk sensitively about students' personal concerns as well academic issues. It was felt he was providing good support and that to expect any more from him in the way of understanding would be to ask for near perfection. With regard to leadership, although they felt he could improve this by being more organised, the fact that he seemed to know what he was doing (and ensured that they knew too by recapping each time on what had been covered previously) gave them a sense of being taught well. His use of sarcasm (Dissatisfied) was, on the whole, seen as a positive aspect of his nature. It was used in a fun way which made the lessons less boring and he permitted the students to give as good as they got, also allowing them to say when they had had enough. However, whilst the general feeling was that his use of sarcasm was acceptable, one student admitted that one occasion had been too close to the mark and another mentioned that it was sometimes used to put them in their place.

The expansion of the students' original Questionnaire responses through these discussions provided the teacher with extra comments to reflect on. His initial decision was to take no action since his communication style seemed relatively positive in his own and the students' perceptions. He felt that to offer more understanding was likely to lead to a loss of focus and timing of lessons or see him becoming a counsellor rather than a teacher. He hoped the situation with regard to leadership would naturally resolve itself the following year when more time would be available for preparation and better organisation once he had completed his teacher training course and discontinued running another class. He considered that sarcasm was so entrenched in not just his style of teaching but also his personality that to alter it on the basis of one negative incident would be inappropriate.

However, some months after these reflections, a slightly different situation emerged. Through noting the occasional hurt his sarcasm had caused, he had become more self-conscious about his use of it. Consequently, he thought he was being less sarcastic than before. An unintentional response to the communication style feedback was being implemented simply because his awareness of a potential barrier to learning had been heightened.

Three teachers of students with mild learning and behavioural difficulties

Three teachers of Vocational Access students used the CSQ to reflect on their own practices when interacting with learners who have mild learning and behavioural difficulties. In addition to using the CSQ, the teachers each had one of their lessons videoed so that the lesson could be reviewed with the students. They intended that the knowledge gained would help to improve learning and teaching practices.

Research by Harkin (1998) indicating that the 'affective' domain in the post-compulsory classroom has a powerful impact on students' learning had influenced the teachers' decision to investigate their styles of communicating with these students. Students want teachers to show friendliness and understanding and to treat them with the respect due to young adults. The communication styles of the teachers working with these students would have a fundamental impact on the students' ability to overcome or manage their learning difficulties, and on their in-classroom behaviour. It was thought that the sharing of teaching strategies among teachers, and sharing of experiences between students and teachers, would be enlightening and of potential benefit to all involved.

The three teachers were all experienced and taught Communications and Numeracy, Information Technology, and Media respectively. The students were generally low academic achievers who need more time in which to develop their skills before seeking employment.

The Communications and Numeracy teacher

The Communications and Numeracy teacher discovered little difference between her self-perceptions and the students' perceptions. During the video feedback session, students were initially looking for 'mistakes' and 'put downs' until they were re-assured that this was not a critical video. They found it very difficult to discuss their feelings about the lesson and the normal dialogue between teacher and students, and the normal self-disclosure between both suddenly dried up until one student asked the teacher how *she* had felt. She was able to explain that, for example, when two people called for her attention at once, she felt confused.

One (particularly difficult) student stayed behind to discuss his feelings with the teacher. He explored with the teacher what he felt when people offered to help him or when they asked him to do something. In turn, the teacher was able to explain her feelings and concerns about his sometimes angry reactions, and a plan of action to move forward was agreed. This improved his relationship with the teacher, which became more founded on an open understanding of each others' feelings.

The Information Technology teacher

There were some marked differences on some scales between the teacher and student perceptions. For example, on the *Understanding* scale, student responses indicated that the teacher may not always be aware when help is needed, and it was this aspect of interaction that was chosen to concentrate on when replaying the video.

During the lesson videoed the atmosphere was one of studious harmony, with occasional teacher–student jokes and student–student jokes; however, a minority of students sat quietly and spent a great deal of time just sitting waiting for the teacher to notice that they needed attention, and seemed quite happy just 'resting'. It was decided that 'seeking help' would be the focus of the video feedback session. The students were asked to identify what different things were happening. They quickly noticed one student asking for attention and they were asked how they felt when they were waiting for attention. No students seemed willing to respond, until the two 'resting' students were asked how they felt. They felt that they would like more attention, if only in the form of praise, and the teacher was pleased to discuss this with them and to plan to pay attention to this in the future. It was decided that, as a group, they would work together on this aspect of communication in their lesson and would discuss it again towards the end of the module.

The Media Studies teacher

There were major differences in the teacher's and students' perceptions of his communication style. An interesting feature that emerged is that on the *Uncertain* scale there were two responses where the students scored 1.8 (1 = Never) and the teacher scored 4 (5 = Always):

- I act as if I do not know what to do.
- It is easy for the students to make a fool out of me.

However, it transpired that both of these are techniques that are used positively by the teacher to help put these students at ease and to generate answers to questions. For example, he often pretends not to know something (*'I act as if I do not know what to do'*) to encourage student participation, and he boosts their self-confidence by allowing them to 'make a fool out of him' (*'Oh no! I haven't got it wrong, have I?'*), but, as the video confirms, this is carried out with humour and does not undermine his leadership. He was not conscious of his *leadership* qualities when he completed the CSQ, but on reflection recognised this as one of his strengths. The video was particularly useful in showing him that, in reality, he demonstrated most of the qualities of *understanding* listed in the Questionnaire, despite low scores for his own self-perception.

What did the three teachers learn together?

Use of the CSQ and of video observation with feedback demonstrated that, as found in a Further Education Funding Council inspection, there did appear to be a good relationship between students and teachers in each of these classes. Mutual respect was demonstrated by the use of adult–adult language, and goodwill was developed by the teachers by such behaviours as showing enthusiasm, allowing some self-disclosure and some laughing and joking.

The use of video recordings to explore features of classroom interaction that had been highlighted by the use of the CSQ was very useful in helping teachers to reflect in more detail about their styles of teaching and self-perceptions. For example, a video recording of a student sitting doing nothing is quite specific and more noticeable than in the general run of a lesson. Similarly, an outburst of student aggression, when viewed in context, can be reflected upon, rather than reacted to.

All three teachers felt that this project had been a very useful exercise, helping them to focus on specific areas of interaction in their classroom and to *'reduce the fear of inspection'* (Media teacher). Additionally, each teacher discovered an area of classroom interaction on which to focus their development:

The Media teacher felt that it had helped him focus on his teaching in a way he had not done for some time. He found the results encouraging and confidence-boosting and felt that this study provided more 'scientific' evidence of his strengths whilst giving him specific behaviours to develop. The Information Technology teacher felt very encouraged with the results and worked on developing her students' skills in being more assertive when they need help. The Communications and Numeracy teacher felt that, although it was not perceived as a problem, her classes were generally noisier than the other two. This is possibly because hers is the only 'workshop' style of class, but it is something she chose to monitor. She also gained insight into other teachers' communication styles which provided much material for reflection on how to increase her own repertoire of teaching behaviours. Use of the CSQ and video developed further the open communication between the teachers on the course and was felt to be a valuable step in their continued professional development.

The College offered participation to all staff and many took up the offer. It is clear that team approaches are important in providing students with a satisfactory learning experience and the team may be enhanced by working together to investigate their styles of communicating with learners.

8 The Communication Styles Questionnaire

The development of a Communications Styles Questionnaire (CSQ) for teachers was considered worthwhile in order to provide teachers with:

- a reliable and valid means of feedback about how they tend to communicate with a particular group of learners, possibly as a basis for joint learner–teacher discussion about classroom interaction;
- detailed information to help them, if they wish, to develop a wider repertoire of communication styles;
- a way of judging whether sufficient opportunities are being created for learners to develop key skills, such as communication and working with others, and to develop learner autonomy.

Background to the CSQ

The Brookes Project is linked to concepts of reflective practice (Dewey, 1933; Schön, 1983, 1987; Kolb, 1984). Many training programmes for teachers claim to be based on a reflective practice model; however, what this means may vary greatly. In particular, it is difficult for teachers, and anyone else, to move beyond 'technical' reflection to 'critical' reflection. Teachers understandably may be unable to stand outside their own perceptions of how they tend to teach; they may also lack a vocabulary that is adequate to describe and discuss how they tend to interact with learners. The CSQ is intended to provide teachers with such a vocabulary, and to provide them with a standpoint on their normal pattern of interaction with a group of students that will enable them to be self-reflective, in a way that goes beyond technical reflection or description.

The CSQ is also linked to action research (Lewin, 1946, 1952; Carr and Kemmis, 1986; Carr, 1995), and a desire to help teachers to research their practices for themselves. Once again, action research is often claimed to be the basis of many staff development programmes for teachers but, when it comes to looking at classroom interaction, it may be very difficult for teachers to obtain accurate insight into their routine styles of communicating with learners. It is possible but costly and time consuming to set up video cameras but they may not record 'routine' patterns of interaction because their presence in a room can distort communication. By contrast, the CSQ records the views of the teacher and all the students to uncover shared understandings and areas of difference about the routine pattern of interaction.

The CSQ is linked to the concept of communicative action (Habermas, 1984, 1987b). Briefly, the possibility of human community is grounded in language use. Our sophisticated use of language is an important characteristic of our humanity. Language is what binds us together in community, and also very often divides us. Only through language is there the possibility of human beings reaching shared understandings and consensus about how life should be lived. In broad, political terms, who is allowed to speak? Who holds the power of decision making and to whom do they listen? How do you give efficacy to the concept of democracy? At a more micro level, which people control language use in everyday interaction? Who determines what can be spoken of and by whom and for how long? Who is listened to? In education, if teachers and young adult learners are to reach a consensus about what should be learned and how; about what should be assessed and how; and if learners are to be engaged personally in this process, then it is only through language use that this will happen.

Development of the CSQ

The CSQ was developed from the Questionnaire on Teacher Interaction (QTI) developed by Wubbels and Levy (1993) at the University of Utrecht. The process of developing the CSQ is detailed in Harkin *et al.* (1999). The study of interaction in the classroom, through which the CSQ was developed, was carried out in naturalistic ways, such as advocated by Barnes (1969, 1984) and Swann (1992). This was intended to yield insights into the social meaning of language in post-compulsory education, in ways that were thought useful by teachers themselves. As well as statistical validation of the CSQ by factor and other analyses, classroom observation took place by videoing whole lessons, to ensure that the CSQ really does accurately reflect normal patterns of teacher–learner interaction. The videos were then reviewed for sequences of interaction between teacher and students that seemed worthy of discussion by the participants, without imposing prior categories.

A questionnaire is a relatively unthreatening means of evaluating interaction because it seems 'out there', as one teacher expressed it, 'scientific'. It seems to give unbiased, objective knowledge of complex, subjective experiences. Of course, no such claims are made for the CSQ. On the contrary, it is recognised that human communication and interaction are highly subjective and the results of the CSQ should be used as a stimulus to sensitive discussion and reflection of what the results may mean, in the perception of participants. We take the view of Harré (1998) that a questionnaire is an 'invitation to a conversation'.

The CSQ is intended to be used voluntarily by teachers – either individually or with colleagues as a team – to gauge how they tend to interact with learners, and whether and to what extent these interactions are regarded positively by students and the teacher. The perceptions of students are not privileged over those of the teacher; nor those of the teacher above the students' views. Human communication is taken to be a plastic, dynamic process, not controlled in an absolute sense by any participant. It is an interactive process in which small decisions of the teacher may affect the feelings of certain learners who in turn will react in ways that affect others in the group, which in turn will influence the teacher, and so on in a complex interplay of interpersonal communication.

It is important that loss of face is avoided in most human interactions (clowning is an exception). Both teachers and learners present 'face' to the world that should be respected. The use of the CSQ, by many teachers and their students, has shown that it is possible to improve everyone's understanding of learner–teacher interaction without anyone losing face. In fact, it is far more likely to lead to enhanced mutual respect, as the veils fall from eyes and teachers and learners see themselves as human beings engaged in a mutual process.

Evaluations of using the CSQ

Evaluations of using the CSQ, by both teachers and students, have been very positive. The involvement of students and teachers *together* in discussing the process of learning has led to useful outcomes, such as designing better assignments, increased understanding of assessment, and improved ethos for learning through greater mutual understanding.

Teachers have found it more useful to be involved in researching their own practices with their students than attending staff development meetings that deal with more general issues. They have variously said that it is helpful to be reminded of the basics of teacher–student communication; that it is useful to take part in discussions with students; and that use of the CSQ has raised issues that they need to discuss with colleagues.

It has sometimes been asked if use of the CSQ improves learning in ways that can be shown through assessment results. There are so many variables involved in educational achievement (e.g. social class, environment, previous achievement, subject, ability, group dynamics, etc.) that causal relationships are unlikely to be established. If teachers and learners *think* that teaching and learning has been improved then this alone is taken to be a positive outcome. If it were possible, through a large-scale, longitudinal study to show conclusively that there are also improvements in assessment results then this would be a bonus. We have seen, however, that mutually supportive, 'warm' relationships lie at the heart of much teaching of young adults. If use of the CSQ improves the quality of relationships then this alone makes its use worthwhile. It is likely that this in turn will lead to improved retention and achievement but no grand claims can be made without more evidence.

How to use the CSQ

The CSQ should not normally be used until after the first month or so of a teacher's work with a student group, by which time a routine or normal communication style should have become established.

Use of the CSQ is beneficial to individual teachers but also to groups of teachers working with a particular group or groups of students who wish to develop their team approach to communication styles. The CSQ results for an individual teacher may depend in part on the teaching styles of colleagues in contact with the students, since students may judge behaviour relative to their other experiences of learning. The questionnaire may be of most use, therefore, when used collaboratively by small groups of colleagues interested in developing their teaching styles together. By working with colleagues, teachers who wish to develop their communication styles can benefit from the group's wider experiences and mutual support.

It is important that feedback from use of the CSQ is sensitive to context, including the constraints upon the way that teachers may communicate. Teachers are not free to interact with learners in any way they wish. Communication is an interactive process and learners, as well as teachers, determine what is possible in a particular situation. Teachers may review their CSQ results alone but more interesting and probing insights are gained from looking at the results with a colleague, preferably one who has been trained in the use of the CSQ and interpreting its results sensitively. When teams of staff each use the CSQ, very useful discussions may take place of different patterns of communication, even with the same students. It is vital to remember in such discussions that the CSQ does not judge people against a norm and that differences of style are a natural human characterstic. Life would be very boring if we all communicated in the same ways.

As a result of a conversation about the results of using the CSQ, it is possible to identify desired changes in how a teacher communicates with learners. As we saw in the last chapter, these changes should arise from a teacher's own perceptions of desirable professional development, and should be self-directed. Teaching style is something personal to an individual and is rarely susceptible to enforced change. The CSQ helps teachers, in a non-threatening process that is controlled by the teacher, to identify aspects of their teaching style that they themselves identify as suitable for development.

Very often, self-directed professional development is more about relatively small changes in behaviour, rather than attempting fundamental shifts in behaviour that may be quite unattainable. Teachers are formed personalities. Albert Camus suggested that people change only in novels. People can amend or adapt their behaviour but more fundamental change is unlikely. When Saul of Tarsus had his revelation or epiphany and became Paul, the evangelist, he remained the same person, as zealous for Christianity as before he had been zealous in its persecution. Teachers should avoid trying to become different people and focus on relatively small changes in their professional repertoire that may, however, bring about important developments in teaching and learning.

The CSQ may be used by staff developers who run initial or in-service programmes. It may be used for instance as part of modules on classroom inter-action, as a means of helping teachers build a vocabulary and a set of concepts to enable them to reflect quite specifically and critically about how they tend to work with particular learners. The work undertaken by teachers may lead to submitting accounts of the process for assessment. At Oxford Brookes University it has been used in this way very successfully by teachers. Within schools and colleges, staff development officers may use the CSQ as a means of helping staff reflect on how they tend to teach, as a means of self-directed professional development, either for its own sake, or in preparation for inspection. The questionnaire is intended to be used only by *volunteer* teachers, because in our opinion it is unethical to force teachers to use it and under involuntary conditions it is highly unlikely that positive professional development will occur.

The fact that it is possible to illuminate a teacher's communication style should not be the endpoint of the enquiry but should be the beginning of a process of self-directed professional development. Teachers are enabled to reflect on their dominant teaching styles in a way that opens the possibility of developing a broader, more flexible repertoire of communication styles. This may best be accomplished in a supportive and encouraging environment in which to attempt new ways of working. Creating such an environment will mean dealing with some of the current practices which make adopting different teaching styles daunting, such as:

- the pressures on the time of teachers and learners, which makes the notions of reflection, discussion, planning and action attractive in theory but very difficult in practice;
- the lack of priority given to the development of teacher's professional teaching skills, as distinct from subject knowledge or management of the curriculum and assessment;
- many students having no formal mechanism for raising, discussing and resolving issues of learning and teaching directly with teachers.

If managers and staff developers can address these issues, to allow time and opportunity for reflective practice, by teachers individually and within teams, then everyone involved should benefit. From the teacher's perspective, the process will enhance personal and professional development and increase the ability to adapt to a variety of new situations and new students. From the students' perspective this may lead to the most appropriate teaching being experienced more uniformly across all areas of the curriculum, being given more opportunities to develop personal autonomy and a range of important key skills. For both teachers and learners, the experience should lead to more enjoyable and more fruitful and fulfilling paterns of working together. From the perspective of institutions, the process will lead to an improved ethos for learning, in which it may become the norm for important issues of teaching and learning to be discussed openly.

Do you wish to use the CSQ?

If teachers, teacher trainers, or staff development officers are interested in being trained to use the CSQ, please contact Dr Joe Harkin at Oxford Brookes University, jcharkin@brookes.ac.uk.

The views of other researchers are also sought about any aspect of this work, regardless of the paradigms of research that they favour.

9 Towards a philosophy of working with young adults

Deep-seated forces compel changes to education practice. There are calls for a 'connective' curriculum, by which is meant the engagement of the learning process with the learner's past experience, present needs and future intentions (Young *et al.*, 1995); an education that requires the commitment, as distinct from the involvement, of learners.

Such a vision of the future of post-14 education chimes with the concern to foster broad-based qualifications that allow all people to develop personal talents that will benefit themselves and their society. It is essential that learners are capable of talking to a purpose, of negotiating, of taking responsibility for their own learning. In contradistinction to this, so much research shows that, even in the 'best' learner–teacher interaction, there is not much student negotiating of learning goals or personal responsibility for learning, or talk to a purpose (as distinct from off-task chatting).

Education systems reflect the nature of the society in which they exist. Their deficiencies are in micro the deficiencies of the wider society of which they form a part. When young people fail to become literate, or drop out of school prematurely there are often societal factors at play, such as poverty, unemployment, and deprivation. Schools and teachers may be blamed for it is convenient to governments that this should be so, and there are failing teachers and failing schools, but a fundamental link between the nature of a society and the nature of its education provision is demonstrable. It is important, therefore, to ask what sort of society would constitute a 'good' society? For in answering this question we cast light on what we would take to be a 'good' education.

The answer to this question varies across time and place but Rorty (1999), following Dewey, believes that Western liberal democracy, at least in its ideals as distinct from its reality, is about as good a society as the world has ever known. This may be gauged pragmatically by a relatively free press, or the average per capita income, or the fact that so many people outside the West would like to move there, or the popularity of Western clothes, drinks, food, and music. It does not follow, of course, that these societies are perfect. They have very many faults but these are open to public debate and potentially, through a democratic political process, to redress.

If we take as a hypothetical starting point when discussing a 'good' education in the UK that it should reflect the ideals of Western liberal democracy, upon what democratic principles should that education be based? Following Dewey (1933), it should be experiential, in the sense of engaging the interests of the learner; it should be reflective, in encouraging people not just to gather facts but to make connections and to critique knowledge. Following Habermas (1986, 1987a) – and Rorty to an extent – it should allow relatively open communication, free as far as possible from domination.

Habermas distinguishes internal and external features of communication. Internal features include that what we say is comprehensible, true, right and sincere. This co-operative view of language is supported by other commentators (Grice, 1975; Aitchison, 1996). External features, such as who has the power to determine what can be talked about, and who is privileged to speak, systematic-ally distort the internal, communicative features of language. In education it is easy to see that teachers have a powerful role in controlling the externals of communication. You do not have an ideal speech situation, although the ideal may always be rare or impossible. That is why it is an ideal.

It is important to evaluate whether educational experience, in a Western liberal democracy such as the UK, tends towards or away from open communication. Is there an acknowledged endeavour to create relatively open communication between teachers and young adult learners? If not, we should question the health and the sustainability of our democracy. Education that reflects, promotes and sustains a democratic society will have democratic features, such as relatively open classrooms, relatively autonomous learners, and attention to the Deweyan emphases on experience and reflection. In turn, the valuing of certain kinds of learning experience gives rise to particular kinds of teaching, in which teachers shape knowledge for the benefit of learners in ways that help them to co-construct knowledge for themselves.

Experienced learners have a sound grasp of these features of teaching, as we have seen in the way that they evaluate their teachers. Some teachers find it difficult to believe that teenagers can give sensitive and delicately balanced opinions about the nature of teaching. The extensive research upon which this book is based shows that learners on all types of programmes are perfectly capable of communicating accurately and sensitively. The surprise is that they are given so few opportunities to voice their opinions.

The possibility of human beings agreeing about anything, including what constitutes a 'good' society, a 'good' education, or 'good' teaching, is vested in language use (Habermas, 1980) and is the fundamental principle upon which Western liberal democracies and democratic education are based. At least three different conceptions of language use may be identified: language as conduit; language as game; language as communication.

Reddy (1979) showed how language is far more than a conduit or means of passing information from A to B. As we have seen, language use is primarily about *warmth* or social bonding, even or perhaps especially in education. Aitchison (1996) pointed out that in fact language is not very good at conveying information – maps, diagrams, and pictures are often better – but is very good at linking people socially. Indeed, Aitchison records that language may have evolved once human groups reached too great a size for physical grooming to bind them together.

Lyotard (1984) stressed a different conception of language that emphasises difference, agonistic challenge and game. Even 'In the ordinary use of discourse – for example, in a discussion between two friends – the interlocutors use any available ammunition . . . questions, requests, assertions, and narratives are launched pell-mell into battle' (p. 17). For Lyotard, human language use is a war.

Habermas (1980, 1986) holds to a more *communicative* and *convivial* conception of language:

> The human interest in autonomy and responsibility is not mere fancy . . . what raises us out of nature is the only thing whose nature we can know: language. Through its structure, autonomy and responsibility are posited for us. Our first sentence expresses unequivocally the intention of universal and unconstrained consensus.
>
> Habermas, 1980

It is important to acknowledge the communicative nature of language in all areas of democratic life. This is particularly important in education where communities of people, drawn often from different backgrounds, come together for a common endeavour. For some teachers and learners language use may be a war, in which games are played, including oppressive discourses of teacher control, and self-protecting games of student disaffection and revolt. However, this is not the practice in most classrooms, especially in post-16 education, where most interaction may follow the adult-to-adult conventions of language use (Catan *et al.*, 1996). Following Habermas, it is clear that we are far from establishing an ideal speech community but importantly we should be endeavouring to make classrooms more open in language practices.

Giddens (1991a) compares the modern world to a juggernaut running out of control. Technology, employment practices, music, clothes, and so much else change so quickly and nobody seems to be in control. Even governments seem caught up in events beyond their comprehension. Within education, young people are under more pressure than ever to succeed in getting higher and better qualifications so that they can stand a chance of hanging on to the juggernaut. In a later work, Giddens (1994) agrees with Rorty that the breaking down of old certainties opens the possibility of 'a cosmopolitan conversation of humankind', and he identifies only four ways in which human beings can resolve disputes: *embedding of tradition*, which in modernity is undermined; *disengagement*, the possibilities of which are limited; *discourse*; or *violence*.

Education should be rooted firmly in a discourse or communicative view of language. This is not to be complacent about how open and communicative educational practices actually are, or may become. Differences of gender, culture and outlook should be celebrated as part of a democratic endeavour. However, it should be acknowledged that there is more that unites human beings, at a fundamental level, than divides us.

Habermas holds that, after Descartes, we took a wrong turn in the road of Enlightenment, asking 'How can I know that something is true?' rather than 'How can members of a community come to an agreement that something is true?' He believes that there should be a revival of the public sphere of democratic decision making, based on communication free from domination.

We need to hold a concept of the ideal speech community in order to form judgements about our society and about education as a feature of society.

A healthy democracy should prepare for participation *through* participation. At what age should young people be encouraged to take part in a dialogue about education and training in which their views are taken seriously? At 3, when they have a sophisticated grasp of language use, including equivocation (Swann, 1992)? At 8, when according to the Catholic Church they have reached the age of reason? At 14, when they are young adults who have reached puberty and may procreate? At 18, when in the UK they may vote? Or later still when they are deemed to be 'adult'?

Surely the practice of democratic participation should begin as early as possible? Just as we expect that studies in all subjects will deepen with age and experience, there is no reason that the participative process of education should not begin at the earliest possible age and deepen towards maturity.

Unfortunately, even an approximation to an ideal speech community does not exist in education, not even in Western liberal democracies. As Darling-Hammond (1996) pointed out in the United States, and many studies have shown in the UK (Barnes, 1969; Rutter *et al.*, 1979; Bennett *et al.*, 1984; Rodenburg, 1992; Keys and Fernandez, 1993) many learners are relatively passive recipients of teaching, even when they are organised in groups for activities. The report of the advisory Group on Education for Citizenship and the teaching of Democracy in Schools (QCA, 1998), focused on an injection of 'subject' knowledge, rather than upon any change in the process of education. Coffield (1998) asked, 'how likely is it that students will become politically literate, socially and morally responsible and active as citizens, if their teachers do not experience and practice democracy in schools?' Young (1992) pointed out that in much educational practice students 'are seen as individuals who must simply be made to reproduce the point of view being advanced, by whatever means seem expedient and economical. This is already well on the way to treating students like things.'

The silence of even young adult learners is profound. This may indicate that there is something terminally wrong with our education system which may be a portent that, if we are not careful, there is something deeply amiss with our democracy too. Rorty believes that within a hundred years it is unlikely that we will still have liberal democracies. I hope that he is wrong and I believe that the practice of education along democratic processes is one way to keep democracy alive. It is important to travel hopefully. To endeavour to make classrooms more participative places that model democracy. To acknowledge that there is more that unites people than divides us and that the basis of this fundamental unity lies in communicative language use, as distinct from language used for domination.

Learners' views and voices have been notably absent from debates about the nature of education, although this is beginning to change (Bloomer and Hodkinson, 1999; Martinez and Munday, 1998; Harkin, 1998). Even a government minister stated (Smith, 2000) that, 'listening to children will help us to get [education] right.' Bentley (1988) argues that if we want education to be effective, 'adult society must take up an active partnership with the people who so far have been largely left out of the debate: with young learners themselves.' He suggests two crucial tests of an effective education system: how well students can apply what they learn beyond education; and how well prepared they are to continue learning throughout life. To succeed in these goals, education should be broader and deeper than it is at present: broader, in the sense of offering a wider range of learning experiences, including those that are valued outside education; and deeper, in the sense of nurturing, 'a greater understanding in young people: understanding of themselves, their motivations and goals in life, and of the subjects and disciplines they study'. This implies an opening out of education to the wider community and chimes with Coffield's belief (1999), from the Learning Society projects, that we have tended to underestimate the importance of informal learning in the formation of skills and knowledge.

Young adult learners generally have little say in what or how they are taught. This is especially so for younger students and part time students. If teaching and learning processes and learners and their needs are to be a central focus of education policy and practice, then it is important to have mechanisms to hear the voices of learners as part of the routine, on-going work of schools, colleges and universities. The CSQ is a valid and reliable means that teachers may use *with their students* to evaluate how they tend routinely to interact and to gauge their experience of education. Its use may introduce a common vocabulary for teachers and learners to share their understandings of what ought to be a common community of interest in learning. Perhaps the climate of education is changing. Interestingly, *Connexions* (DfEE, 2000d) intends to bring together several government departments, and to listen to young people themselves, to try to raise retention and achievement. Perhaps the days when the experience of being educated in a 'public' (i.e. private) school and a state school or college will not persist in being so different?

Rodenburg (1992) compared the use of language in a comprehensive to that at Eton: whereas in the latter students discussed freely in class, in the comprehensive a silence prevailed that amounted almost to verbal deprivation. Some, more privileged young people already experience high levels of personal autonomy and democratic education; while others are treated as 'hands'. The concept of 'empowerment' of learners, as Hodkinson (1995) has shown, has overlapping dimensions that should be recognised if it is to be more than a rhetorical expression. These elements include personal effectiveness, critical autonomy and what Hodkinson calls 'community' – a collective empowerment that sits well with Habermas's idea of situated reason.

Young people, more than ever before, can obtain knowledge from electronic sources and libraries; what they need are educational settings in which they can interact with teachers and with one another to learn the human significance of this knowledge and, at the same time, to learn about themselves and about difference and tolerance. Education requires more than a Kantian treating of persons as ends in themselves; it requires the affirmation of the person as a person, in a process which balances personal and rational autonomy with the fact that the everyday life of humans is one of *coexistence*.

The development of key skills in communication integrated across the curriculum is one means of developing a 'connective' curriculum that encourages more commitment by students to the process of learning. A more communicative classroom, based on the use of a broader, more open repertoire of language, may make possible more equitable relations between people and provide a surer foundation for a healthy, democratic society.

As Kingman (1988) declared:

> People need expertise in language to be able to participate effectively in a democracy . . . A democratic society needs people who have the linguistic abilities which will enable them to discuss, evaluate and make sense of what they are told, as well as to take effective action on the basis of their understanding . . . Otherwise there can be no genuine participation, but only the imposition of the ideas of those who are linguistically capable.

Silver (1999), in considering 'learning for futures', points to the central role of educators in shaping education to the principles of democracy. He posed the question, 'How do [teachers] interpret their roles in the profoundly changing contours of "community"? . . . Education is *now* deeply involved with democratic principles and moral values.' It is difficult to predict the future role of teachers, except to say that what is taking shape is a 'greater independence and self-direction in learning. Both of these relate back to the emphasis on "community" or "co-operative" learning.'

Recent reports underline a need to improve the communicative competence of young people as a foundation for many aspects of life. An ALBSU report (1995) showed a very strong correlation between low basic skills of parents and low attainment of children. The Report stated that the link is particularly strong for literacy skills and shows that failure to develop communication skills in one generation will certainly harm the next.

Walker (1995) showed that communication failure in Britain is very costly in terms of the breakdown of relationships, ill health, and lost productivity. The ability to speak does not automatically mean an ability to communicate effectively – as anyone knows who reflects on such things as the difficulties some students have in grasping particular subjects or concepts because of misunderstandings of language, rather than lack of ability; and the conflicts and emotional tangles caused in personal relationships by failure to speak assertively or to really listen. According to the DfEE (2000c), 'Research and surveys consistently conclude that it is [improving own learning and performance, and problem solving] plus oral communication which employers value most.'

Two contrasting views of education may be identified. One in which education is seen as a process of evolving as an autonomous human being through structured support. Education provides frameworks of opportunity and resources, human and physical, to allow each individual to benefit from a complex series of engagements with learning that is moral, spiritual, intellectual, physical, creative and social. This scenario is about *entitlement* and about the interrelation of all the experiences which contribute ultimately to the adult state. The rewards are intrinsic, the goals are personal and the values are embedded in the very core of the individual's existence. There is parity of esteem between goals so that no one interpretation of goal is dominant, leaving room for academic, vocational, creative and practical goals to coexist within a broad and balanced spectrum of education.

An alternative view of education elevates intellectual behaviour above other learning. The means by which education is evaluated is by standard attainment targets and similar tests post-16. Learners are graded according to their ability to satisfy, at certain ages in their life, the tests which adults have devised for them. This view of learning is rooted in a belief that education should demonstrate value to gross national product through the measurement of higher and higher attainment in a narrow range of learning outcomes.

In the first view of education, there is room for the views of learners to be raised in a conversation about their perceptions of learning needs. The second view tightly circumscribes teachers and learners in the low trust delivery of other people's visions of what learners need.

The first view of education creates the conditions in which learners and teachers may cooperate. It focuses on the fact that the relationship between the teacher and the learner is central to the success of the learning process.

The views of the Fryer Report (1997) on lifelong learning bear repeating, that institutional and management structures in education have for too long been the central concern of policy makers and administrators. These structures should serve the needs of learners and teachers and not become ends in themselves. It is learning and teaching that is central to education, not administration and management.

In the 1995 Frederick Constable lecture at the Royal Society of Arts, Ruth Silver, a college principal, criticised a:

> ... funding methodology that drives providers towards qualifications rather than towards something which values what students and teachers between them construct as a valuable, marketable learning experience.

If there is a coherent message about the teaching of all young adults, and not just the most cooperative, it is that:

- Teachers who show leadership which is social, open and relatively democratic are more effective in turning round disaffected learners.
- The life history of each individual can be seen as an asset to the teacher, if learner experience and natural learning style is the starting point for teaching.

- The teacher's role is to plan learning approaches which gradually enable the learner to accommodate to different styles of learning and to new knowledge.
- Learning is most effective when motivation is more intrinsic than extrinsic, when learners enjoy learning because they find it stimulating and more than a passport to the next stage in their lives.
- Intrinsic motivation is built on a high level of trust between teacher and learner, in which there is mutual respect and relatively open patterns of communication.

The grand paradox

Much of what passes for 'education' is dull and of little relevance to learners. We know a great deal about the nature of effective learning and could bring about profound improvements in education by putting what we know about learning and learners into effect. That we fail to do this, despite the Rousseaus, Deweys, and Stenhouses of the world is testimony to the tenacity of bad habit and entrenched interests. Habit, as one of the main characters in *Waiting for Godot* says, is a great deadener. Managers, teachers and learners are habituated to current practice, even the ghastly bits. There exists an uncomfortable equilibrium by which teachers and learners together agree to hold tenaciously to the present arrangements for education. It is easier than making profound changes. The 'better' students, in any case, are doing relatively well as a result of chalk and talk and skills and drills. The 'weaker' students have long since given up hope that education will change. They want out and many, even before the statutory leaving age, have already left. For their part, managers are so busy managing budgets and fire fighting a fundamentally ineffective educational structure that they have little energy to look at learning and teaching. Unless something goes drastically wrong, or unless there is an Ofsted inspection coming up, teaching, teachers and learners are expected to just get on with the job. At best the job of managers is to obtain maximum benefit from the present educational arrangements. There is also Vainhinger's law which states that, in any system, the means will preponderate over the ends. Systems for the efficient delivery of education rapidly become self-serving. All this is made possible by confusions in national policy for education and training. One policy statement talks of key skills, empowering learners, encouraging learner autonomy and so on; another talks of discipline, back to basics and good, old fashioned skills and drills, whole class teaching. In the interstices of such confusion, for managers and teachers it is business as usual.

It is time to build a high-trust, democratic education system that respects learners and their experiences, listens closely to their expressions of interest and need, builds partnerships between teachers, learners, parents, the community, and employers so that young adults learn what they wish to learn, when they wish to learn, and how they wish to learn. Some will not learn in this relatively open system – but many do not learn in our present relatively closed one. There should be opportunities for people to opt back in to education when they are ready and, without the deep scars caused by education at present, it is likely that many would opt in at a later date.

Neither the teaching profession, except for a few exceptional individuals, nor the education hierarchy will willingly change the present education system. For all sorts of reasons, there are far too many vested interests in maintaining the status quo. What and where then are the levers of change? Perhaps in the too long silenced and marginalised voices of learners themselves.

The entry into post-compulsory education of many young adults as the *de facto* leaving age ceases to be 16, and further and higher education continue to expand, may be seen as a threat to standards and to the present educational equilibrium. If, however, these 'new' learners are seen as an asset, bringing to education a range of life experiences that may not be as middle class as those of most people who have traditionally entered post-compulsory education, then perhaps they will be the catalyst for fundamental change in education. Not content to receive more of what they have already endured with indifference or hostility, they may challenge educationalists to provide an experience which promotes rational autonomy, personal engagement and a healthy social democracy.

Appendix

Teacher questionnaire (FE: Actual)

1 I talk enthusiastically about the subject
2 I am friendly
3 I give the students opportunities to contribute their opinions
4 I give work that is too easy to do
5 I give the students opportunities to share their views with each other

6 I expect the students to decide how they allocate their time to each topic
7 I explain things clearly
8 I expect the students to keep up with the demands of the course
9 The students can change my mind
10 I am lenient in marking work

11 I think that the students know very little
12 The students have to be silent in my class
13 I hold the students' attention
14 I can take a joke
15 I allow the students to work at their own pace

16 I expect the students to assess their own work
17 I put the students down
18 The students are afraid of me
19 I know everything that goes on in the room
20 I allow the students to assess each others work

21 The students have the opportunity to choose the assignments they work on
22 I set a lot of homework
23 I am patient
24 The students need my permission before they speak
25 I am well organised

26 I assess the students' work fairly

27 I allow the students choice in what they study
28 I let the students work at a slow pace
29 I appear dissatisfied with the students
30 The students feel uneasy about asking me questions

31 I act confidently
32 I let the students make a lot of noise
33 I let the students present their work to the class
34 I pretend not to notice when the students fool around
35 I have a low opinion of the students

36 The students feel uneasy about speaking to each other in my class
37 I help the students with their work
38 I trust the students
39 I let the students fool around in class
40 I am sarcastic

41 I get angry unexpectedly
42 I set hard work
43 I am someone the students can depend on
44 If the students disagree with me, we can talk about it
45 I let the students get away with a lot in class

46 I act as if I do not know what to do
47 I get angry quickly
48 My standards are high
49 I am uninterested in the subject
50 I am willing to explain things again

51 I demand that work is handed in on time
52 I let the students boss me around
53 The students can talk to me about things other than work
54 I provide the students with useful feedback
55 I let the students research for themselves

56 If the students have something to say I will listen
57 I let the students talk about anything in class
58 I am not sure what to do when the students fool around
59 I am impatient
60 The students' attention wanders when I am talking

61 It takes a lot of effort to do the work I set
62 It is easy for the students to make a fool out of me
63 It is easy for the students to pick a fight with me
64 I am disappointed if the students don't do their best

This questionnaire was developed from the Questionnaire on Teacher Interaction developed by Theo Wubbels and Jack Levy, 1993. It is accompanied in use by three other questionnaires: Teacher Ideal; Student Actual; Student Ideal. Together the four questionnaires give a view of different perceptions of interaction between a teacher and a particular group of learners.

It is recommended that, before using the CSQ, teachers should be trained in its use so that the results may be interpreted sensitively, as a means of self-directed professional development.

Use of the questionnaire: **If you wish to use the questionnaire, please contact Dr. Joe Harkin, Institute of Education, Oxford Brookes University, Harcourt Hill, Oxford OX2 9AT, UK. jcharkin@brookes.ac.uk.**

Teacher questionnaire (HE: Actual)

1 I talk enthusiastically about the subject
2 I am friendly
3 I give the students opportunities to contribute their opinions
4 I give work that is too easy to do
5 I think the students cheat

6 I am strict
7 I explain things clearly
8 I expect the students to keep up with the demands of the course
9 The students can change my mind
10 I am lenient in marking work

11 I think that the students know very little
12 The students have to be silent in my class
13 I hold the students' attention
14 I can take a joke
15 I allow the students to work at their own pace

16 I put up with work which is not the students' best
17 I put the students down
18 The students are afraid of me
19 I know everything that goes on in the room
20 My class is pleasant

21 The students have the opportunity to choose the assignments they work on
22 It takes only a little effort to do work I set
23 I think that the students do things badly
24 The students need my permission before they speak
25 I am a good leader

26 I assess the students' work fairly
27 I allow the students choice in what they study
28 I let the students work at a slow pace
29 I appear dissatisfied with the students
30 The students do not feel at ease to ask me questions

31 I act confidently
32 The students think of me as one of them
33 I let the students present their work to the class
34 I do not mind if work is handed in late
35 I have a low opinion of the students

36 The students do not feel at ease to speak to each other in my class
37 I help the students with their work
38 I trust the students
39 I give scope for the students to share their views with each other
40 I seem uncertain

41 I get angry unexpectedly
42 I set hard work
43 I am someone the students can depend on
44 If the students don't agree with me, we can talk about it
45 I expect the students to decide how they allocate their time to each topic

46 I act as if I do not know what to do
47 I get angry quickly
48 My standards are high
49 I am uninterested in teaching the subject
50 I am willing to explain things again

51 I am lenient
52 I give in to the students' demands
53 I am too quick to correct the students when they break a rule
54 I provide the students with useful feedback
55 I am severe when marking work

56 If the students have something to say I will listen
57 I expect the students to appraise their own work
58 I am not sure what to do when the students are inattentive
59 I am impatient
60 The students' attention wanders when I am talking

61 It takes a lot of effort to do the work I set
62 I realise when the students don't understand
63 I let the students move around the room without asking permission

64   I give equal help to everyone
65   I expect the students to carry out background reading for my class

66   I am patient
67   I allow the students to assess each others' work
68   I pretend not to notice when the students are inattentive
69   I am sarcastic
70   I demand that work is handed in on time

71   The students can talk to me about things other than work
72   I let the students research for themselves
73   I am disappointed if the students don't do their best

This questionnaire was developed from the Questionnaire on Teacher Inter-action developed by Theo Wubbels and Jack Levy, 1993. It is accompanied in use by three other questionnaires: Teacher Ideal; Student Actual; Student Ideal. Together the four questionnaires give a view of different perceptions of interaction between a teacher and a particular group of learners.

It is recommended that, before using the CSQ, teachers should be trained in its use so that the results may be interpreted sensitively, as a means of self-directed professional development.

Use of the questionnaire: **If you wish to use the questionnaire, please con-tact Dr. Joe Harkin, Institute of Education, Oxford Brookes University, Harcourt Hill, Oxford OX2 9AT, UK. jcharkin@brookes.ac.uk.**

Bibliography

Adams, J. S. (1992) 'Towards an understanding of inequity', in G. Moorhead and R.W. Griffin (eds) *Organizational Behavior*, Boston: Houghton Mifflin Company.

Aitchison, J. (1996) *The Seeds of Speech*, Cambridge: Cambridge University Press.

ALBSU (1995) *Parents and their Children: the Intergenerational Effect of Poor Basic Skills*, London: ALBSU.

Archer, S. (ed.) (1994) *Interventions for Adolescent Identity Development*, London: Sage.

Arendt, H. (1958) *The Human Condition*, Chicago: University of Chicago Press.

Argyle, M. (1982) *The Psychology of Interpersonal Behaviour*, Harmondsworth: Penguin.

Baker, K. (1989) Speech to Association of Colleges of Further and Higher Education, Scarborough, 16 February.

Ball, M. (1998) *School Inclusion: the School, the Family and the Community*, York: Joseph Rowntree Foundation.

Bandura, A. (1978) 'The self system in reciprocal determinism', *American Psychologist* 33: 344–58.

Banks, O. (1976) *The Sociology of Education*, London: Batsford.

Bannister, D. and Fransella, F. (1986) *Inquiring Man: the Psychology of Personal Constructs*, London: Routledge.

Banyard, P. and Hayes, N. (1994) *Psychology: Theory and Application*, London: Chapman & Hall.

Barnes, D. (1969) *Language, the Learner and the School*, Harmondsworth: Penguin.

Barnes, D. (1984) *Versions of English*, London: Heinemann.

Bates, I. (1995) 'The competence movement: conceptualising recent research', *Studies in Science Education* 25: 39–68.

Bates, I. (1997) 'Problematizing "empowerment" in education and work: an exploration of the GNVQ', Leeds: School of Education, Paper 7.

BECTA (1998) *Snapshots of Innovation: a collection of case studies identifying good practice in the use of Information and Learning Technology (ILT) in Colleges*, Coventry: British Educational Communications and Technology Agency (BECTA).

——(1999) *Learning on Line: electronic learning resources in Further Education*, Coventry: British Educational Communications and Technology Agency (BECTA).

Belbin, E., Downs, S. and Perry, P. (1981) *How do I Learn?*, Cambridge: Further Education Unit.

Bennett, N., Desforges, C., Cockburn, A. and Wilkinson, B. (1984) *The Quality of Pupil Learning Experiences*, London: Lawrence Erlbaum.

Bentley, T. (1998) *Learning Beyond the Classroom*, London: Routledge.

Berlak, A. and Berlak, H. (1981) *Dilemmas of Schooling, Teaching and Social Change*, London: Methuen.

Bernstein, B. (1971) *Class, Codes and Control, Vol.1. Theoretical Studies Towards a Sociology of Language*, London: Routledge & Kegan Paul.

Biggs, J. B. (1989) 'Does learning about learning help teachers with teaching?' Psychology and the tertiary teacher, *The Gazette*, 26 (Suppl.) 1, University of Hong Kong.

Bloom, B. S. (1956) *Taxonomy of Educational Objectives, Book 1, Cognitive Domain*, London: Longman.

Bloomer, M. and Hodkinson, P. (1999) *College Life: the Voice of the Learner*, London: FEDA.

Bowkett, S. (1997*) Imagine that: A handbook of Creative Learning Activities for the Classroom*, Stafford: Network Educational Press.

Brandes, D. and Phillips, H. (1979) *The Gamester's Handbook*, London: Hutchinson.

Brekelmans, M. (1994) 'Interpersonal behaviour of teachers in the first decade of their professional careers', paper to the Twentieth Annual Conference of the British Educational Research Association.

Brekelmans, M. and Creton, H. (1993) 'Interpersonal teacher behaviour throughout the career', in T. Wubbels and J. Levy (eds) *Do You Know What You Look Like? Interpersonal Relationships in Education*, London: Falmer.

Brekelmans, M., Wubbels, T. and Levy, J. (1993) 'Student performance, attitudes, instructional strategies and teacher-communication style', in T. Wubbels and J. Levy (eds) *Do You Know What You Look Like?: Interpersonal Relationships in Education*, London: Falmer.

Bruner, J. S. (1966) *Towards a Theory of Instruction*, Cambridge, MA: Harvard University Press.

Bullock, Sir A. (1975) *A Language for Life*, London: HMSO.

Burgess, B. (1983) *Problem Solving at Work*, Lancaster: Framework Press.

——(1986) *Problem Solving at Work: Update*, Lancaster: Framework Press.

Callaghan, J. (1976) Speech at Ruskin College, Oxford, 18 October 1976.

Carlgren, I., Handal, G. and Vaage, S. (eds) (1994) *Teachers' Minds and Actions*, London: Falmer.

Carr, W. (1995) *For Education: Towards Critical Educational Inquiry*, Buckingham: Open University Press.

Carr, W. and Kemmis, S. (1986) *Becoming Critical: Education, Knowledge and Action Research*, Brighton: Falmer Press.

Catan, L., Dennison, C. and Cleman, J. (1996) *Getting Through: Effective Communication in the Teenage Years*, London: The BT Forum.

Child, D. (1993) *Psychology and the Teacher*, London: Cassell.

Chitty, C. (1992) *The Education System Transformed*, Manchester: Baseline Books.

Coffield, F. (ed.) (1997) *A National Strategy for Lifelong Learning*, Newcastle: University of Newcastle.

——(1998a) 'A fresh approach to learning for the learning age: the contribution of research', *Higher Education Digest* 31: 4–6.

——(1998b) 'Four cheers for democracy: citizenship and lifelong learning', in D. Christie, H. Maitles and J. Halliday (eds) *Values Education for Democracy and Citizenship: Proceedings of the Gordon Cook Foundation Conference 1998*, Glasgow: University of Strathclyde.

——(ed.) (1999) *Informal Learning*, Bristol: The Policy Press.

Cohen, R. and Long, S. (1998) 'Children and anti-poverty strategies', *Children and Society* 12(2): 73–85.

Coleman, J. C. and Hendry, L. (1990) *The Nature of Adolescence*, London: Routledge.

Confederation of British Industry (1989) *Towards a Skills Revolution: A Youth Charter*, London: CBI.

Crequer, N. (1996) *For Life: a Vision for Learning in the Twenty-first Century*, London: The Campaign for Learning.

Crowther, Sir G. (1959) *15–18*, London: HMSO.

Dale, E. (1946) *Audio Visual Methods in Teaching*, Illinois: Dryden Press.

Darling-Hammond, L. (1996) 'The right to learn and the advancement of teaching: research, policy, and practice for democratic education', *Educational Researcher* 25(6): 5–17.

Dearing, Sir R. (1996) *Review of Qualifications for 16 to 19-year olds*, London: SCAA.

Dearing, Sir R. (1997) *Higher Education in the Learning Society*, London: HMSO.

Department for Education and Employment (1999a) *Learning To Succeed: A New Framework For Post-16 Learning*, London: HMSO.

Department for Education and Employment (1999b) *Participation in Education and Training by 16–18 Year Olds in England 1988 to 1998*, London: HMSO.

Department for Education and Employment (2000a) Blunkett announces major expansion and reform of vocational learning, http://www.dfee.gov.uk/news.

Department for Education and Employment (2000b) *The National Curriculum; Possible Modifications at Key Stage 4*, http://www.nc.uk.net/about/about.

Department for Education and Employment (2000c) *Key Skills*, http://www.dfee.gov.uk/key.

Department for Education and Employment (2000d) *Connexions: the Best Start in Life for Every Young Person*, London: HMSO.

Department of Education and Science (1991) *Education and Training for the Twenty-first Century*, London: HMSO.

Department of Employment (1990) *Flexible Learning in Schools*, London: HMSO.

Dewey, J. (1933) *How We Think*, Boston: Heath.

—(1963) *Experience and Education*, New York: Collier.

—(1974) *John Dewey on Education: Selected Writings*, Chicago: University of Chicago Press.

Drucker, P. (1969) *The Age of Discontinuity*, New York: Harper & Row.

Eggen, P. D. and Kauchak, D. P. (1988) *Strategies for Teachers: Teaching Content and Thinking Skills*, Englewood Cliffs, NJ: Prentice Hall.

Eggen, P. D., Kauchak, D. P. and Harder, R. J. (1979) *Strategies for Teachers: Information Processing Models in the Classroom*, Englewood Cliffs, NJ: Prentice Hall.

Entwistle, N. (1987) *Understanding Classroom Learning*, London: Hodder & Stoughton.

Entwistle, N. and Ramsden, P. (1983) *Understanding Student Learning*, London: Croom Helm.

Eraut, M. (1994) *Evaluating Professional Knowledge and Competence*, London: Falmer.

Felouzis, G. (1994) Le 'Bon Prof': La construction de l'autorité dans les lycées, *Sociologie du Travail*, 36: 361–376.

Finegold, D. (1993) 'Breaking out of the low skill equilibrium', in *Briefings of the National Commission on Education*, London: Heinemann.

Fryer, R. H. (1997) *Learning for the Twenty-first Century, First Report of the National Advisory Group for Continuing Education and Lifelong Learning*, London: HMSO.

Further Education Development Agency (1998) *Non-Completion Of GNVQs*, London: FEDA.

Further Education Development Agency (2000) 'Curriculum 2000', flyer for a conference on 4 April 2000, London: FEDA.

Further Education Funding Council (1997a) Widening Participation In Further Education: Statistical Evidence, Coventry: FEFC.

Further Education Funding Council (1997b) How To Widen Participation: A Guide To Good Practice, Coventry: FEFC.

Further Education Funding Council (1998), *The Use of Technology to Support Learning in Colleges*, Coventry: FEFC.

Further Education Funding Council (1999) *Quality And Standards In Further Education In England 1997–98*, Chief Inspector's Annual Report, Coventry: FEFC.

Further Education National Training Organisation (1999) S*tandards for Teaching and Supporting Learning in Further Education in England and Wales*, London: FENTO.

Further Education Unit (1991) *Flexible Colleges*, London: FEU.

Further Education Unit (1993) *Principles for the Development of Core Skills Across the Curriculum*, London: FEU.

Gaardner, J. (1995) *Sophie's World*, London: Phoenix House.

Gagné, R. (1975) *Essentials of Learning for Instruction*, Hinsdale, Ill: Dryden Press.

——(1985) *The Conditions of Learning and Theory of Instruction*, London: Holt-Saunders International Editions.

Gagné, R. M., Briggs, L. J. and Wager, W. W. (1994) *Principles of Instructional Design*, London: Holt, Rinehart and Winston.

Gardner, H. (1993) *Frames of Mind: The Theory of Multiple Intelligences*, London: Fontana.

Gauvain, M. and Rogoff, B. (1989) 'Collaborative problem solving and the development of children's planning skills', *Developmental Psychology* 25: 139–51.

Gibbs, G. (1981) *Teaching Students to Learn: a Student-centred Approach*, Milton Keynes: The Open University Press.

——(1988a) *253 Ideas for Alternative Learning Week*, Oxford Brookes University: Educational Methods Unit.

——(1988b) *Learning by Doing: a Guide to Teaching and Learning*, London: Further Education Unit/Longmans.

——(1992) *Improving the Quality of Student Learning*, Bristol: Technical & Educational Services.

Gibbs, G., Habeshaw, S. and Habeshaw, T. (1984*) 53 Interesting Things to do in Your Lectures*, Bristol: Technical and Educational Services.

Giddens, A. (1991a) *The Consequences of Modernity*, Cambridge: Polity Press.

——(1991b) *Modernity and Self-Identity*, Stanford: Stanford University Press.

——(1994) 'Living in a post-traditional society', in U. Beck, A. Giddens and S. Lash (eds) *Reflexive Modernization*, Cambridge: Polity Press.

Goleman, D. (1996) *Emotional Intelligence: Why It Can Matter More than IQ*, London: Bloomsbury.

Greenberg, J. and Baron, R. A. (1993) *Behavior in Organizations*, London: Allyn & Bacon.

Greenhalgh, P. (1994) *Emotional Growth and Learning*, London: Routledge.

Grice, P. (1975) 'Logic and Conversation', in P. Cole and J. Morgan (eds) *Syntax and Semantics, III: Speech Acts*, New York: Academic Press.

Grubb, W. N. (1996) Comments made in a symposium held on 23/24 October 1996, Hanover, Germany on 'The future of training and vocational education in the global economy' in J. Harkin (ed.) *Technological Change, Employment and the Responsiveness of Education and Training Providers, Compare*, 27(1): 113–21.

——(1999) *Honored But Invisible: An Inside Look at Teaching in Community Colleges*, London: Routledge.

Habermas, J. (1980) 'Modernity – an incomplete project', speech on receiving the Adorno prize, Frankfurt, September 1980.

——(1984) *The Theory of Communicative Action, Vol. 1*, London: Heinemann.

——(1986) *Knowledge and Human Interests*, Cambridge: Polity Press.

——(1987a) *The Philosophical Discourse of Modernity*, Cambridge: Polity Press.

——(1987b) *The Theory of Communicative Action, Vol. 2*, Cambridge: Polity Press.

Halsey, A. H., Heath, A. F. and Ridge, J. M. (1980) *Origins and Destinations*, Oxford: Clarendon.

Harkin, J. and Davis, P. (1996a) 'The communication styles of teachers in post-compulsory education', *Journal of Further and Higher Education* 20(1): 25–34.

——(1996b) 'The impact of GNVQs on the communication styles of teachers', *Research in Post-compulsory Education* 1(1): 117–26.

Harkin, J. (1991) 'The development of English and communication in further education', unpublished D.Phil. thesis, University of Sussex.

——(1997) 'Technological change, employment and the responsiveness of education and training providers', *Compare*, 27(1): 113–21.

——(1998) 'Constructs used by students in England and Wales to evaluate their teachers', *Journal of Vocational Education and Training* 50(3): 339–53.

——(1998) 'In defence of the modernist project in education', *British Journal of Educational Studies* 46(4): 404–15.

Harkin, J. and Turner, G. (1997) 'Patterns of communication styles of teachers in English 16–19 education', *Research in Post-Compulsory Education* 2(3): 263–81.

Harkin, J., Davis, P. and Turner, G. (1999) 'The development of a Communication Styles Questionnaire for use in English 16–19 education', *Westminster Studies in Education* 22: 31–47.

Harré (1998) *The Singular Self*, London: Sage.

Herzberg. F. (1968) *Work and the Nature of Man*, London: Crosby, Lockwood Staples.

Higginson, G. R. (1988) *Advancing A Levels*, London: HMSO.

Hirst, P. H. and Peters, R. S. (1970) *The Logic of Education*, London: Routledge & Kegan Paul.

Hodkinson, P. (1995) 'Professionalism and competence', in P. Hodkinson and M. Issitt (eds) *The Challenge of Competence*, London: Cassell.

Holtermann, S. (1996) 'The impact of public expenditure and fiscal policy on Britain's children and young people', *Children and Society* 10(1): 3–13.

Honey, P. and Mumford, A. (1992) *The Manual of Learning Styles*, Maidenhead: Peter Honey.

Hopson, B. and Scally, M. (1980) *Lifeskills Teaching Programmes No. 1*, Leeds: Lifeskills Associates.

Horrocks, J. E. (1976) *The Psychology of Adolescence*, Boston: Houghton Mifflin.

Huczinski, A. A. and Buchanan, D. A. (1985) *Organizational Behaviour*, London: Prentice Hall.

Hyland, T. and Weller, P. (1994) 'Implementing GNVQs in post-16 education', University of Warwick: Continuing Education Research Centre.

——(1996) 'Monitoring GNVQs: a national survey of provision and implementation', *Educational Research* 38: 1.

Jessup, G. (1995) 'Outcome based qualifications and the implications for learning', in J. Burke (ed.) *Outcomes, Learning and the Curriculum*, London: Falmer.

Johannessen, T., Gronhaug, K., Risholm, N. and Mikalsen, O. (1997) 'What is important to students? Exploring dimensions in their evaluations of teachers', *Scandinavian Journal of Educational Research* 41(2): 165–77.

Josselson, R. (1994) 'The theory of identity development and the question of intervention', in S. Archer (ed.) *Interventions for Adolescent Identity Development*, London: Sage.

Kelly, G. (1955) *The Psychology of Personal Constructs*, New York: W.W. Norton.

Keys, W. and Fernandez, C. (1993) *What Do Children Think About School?*, Slough: NFER.

Kingman, Sir J. (1988) *Report of the Committee of Enquiry into the Teaching of the English Language*, London: HMSO.

Klemp, G., Schneider, C. and Kastendiek, S. (1985) 'The balancing act: competencies of effective teachers and mentors', *Innovation Abstracts* V, 4, Austin: University of Texas.

Knowles, M. S. (1970) *The Modern Practice of Adult Education: Andragogy versus Pedagogy*, New York: Association Press.

Kolb, D. A. and Fry, R. (1975) 'Towards an applied theory of experiential learning', in C. L. Cooper (ed.) *Theories of Group Processes*, London: John Wiley & Sons.

Kolb, D. A. (1984) *Experiential Learning: Experience as the Source of Learning and Development*, London: Prentice Hall.

——(1993) 'The process of experiential learning', in M. Thorpe, R. Edwards and A. Hanson (eds) *Culture and Processes of Adult Learning*, London: Routledge/Open University Press.

Leary, T. (1957) *An Interpersonal Diagnosis of Personality*, New York: Ronald Press Company.

Lee, V. and Das Gupta, P. (1995) *Children's Cognitive and Language Development*, Oxford: Blackwell/Open University Press.

Levy, J., Creton, H. and Wubbels, T. (1993) 'Perceptions of interpersonal teacher behaviour', in T. Wubbels and J. Levy (eds) *Do You Know What You Look Like? Interpersonal Relationships in Education*, London: Falmer.

Lewin, K. (1946) 'Action research and minority problems', *Journal of Social Issues* 2(4): 34–6.

——(1988) 'Group decisions and social change', *The Action Research Reader*, Victoria: Deakin University Press.

Light, P. and Glachan, M. (1985) 'Facilitation of individual problem solving through peer interaction', *Educational Psychology* 5: 217–25.

Lucas, N. (1997) 'The changing sixth form: the growth of pre-vocational education', in S. Capel, M. Leask and T. Turner (eds) *Starting to Teach*, London: Routledge.

Lyotard, J.-F. (1984) *The Postmodern Condition: A Report on Knowledge*, Manchester: Manchester University Press.

Maier, H. W. G. (1978) *Three Theories of Child Development*, London: Harper & Row.

Manaster, G. J. (1977) *Adolescent Development and the Life Tasks*, London: Allyn & Bacon.

Martinez, P. and Munday, F. (1998) *9,000 Voices: Student Persistence And Drop Out In Further Education*, London: FEDA.

Marton, F. and Säljö, R. (1976) 'On qualitative differences in learning: I. Outcomes and process', *British Journal of Educational Psychology* 46: 4–11.

Marton, F. (1984) 'Approaches to learning', in F. Marton, D. Hounsell and N. J. Entwistle (eds) *The Experience of Learning*, Edinburgh: Scottish Academic Press.

Maslow, A. (1943) 'A theory of human motivation', *The Psychological Review* 50(4): 370–96.

Maxted, P. (1996) *From the Ivory Tower to the Street: Putting Learning Theory into Practice*, London: The Campaign for Learning.

McClelland, D. (1961) *The Achieving Society*, Princeton: Van Nostrand.

Mitchell, T. R. (1982) 'Motivation: new directions for theory, research and practice', *Academy of Management Review* 7(1): 80–88.

Moorhead, G. and Griffin, R. W. (1992) *Organizational Behavior*, Boston: Houghton Mifflin.

Mullins, L. J. (1999) *Management and Organisational Behaviour*, London: Pitman.

Mumford, A. (1995) *Effective Learning*, London: Institute of Personnel and Development.

National Association of Teachers in Further and Higher Education (1995) 'GNVQ workload is weighing down lecturers', *The Lecturer*, Summer: 3.

National Council for Vocational Qualifications (1989) *Common Learning Outcomes: Core Skills in A/AS Levels and NVQs*, London: NCVQ.

National Curriculum Council (1989) *Core Skills 16–19*, London: NCC.

Newbolt, Sir H. (1921) *The Teaching of English in England*, London: HMSO.

Newstead, S. (1998) 'Individual differences in student motivation', in S. Brown, S. Armstrong and G. Thompson (eds) *Motivating Students*, London: Kogan Page.

National Foundation for Educational Research (1994) Survey into stress in post-compulsory education, *NATFHE Journal*, Autumn: 4–5.

Oates, T. and Harkin, J. (1994) 'From design to delivery: the implementation of the NCVQ core skills units', in J. Burke (ed.) *Outcomes, Learning and the Curriculum: Implications for NVQs, GNVQs and Other Qualifications*, London: Falmer.

O'Donnell, M. B. (1985) *Age and Generation*, London: Tavistock Publications.

Organisation for Economic Cooperation and Development (1978) *Centre for Educational Research and Innovation*, Paris: OECD.

Piaget, J. and Inhelder, B. (1966) *The Psychology of the Child*, London: Routledge & Kegan Paul.

Porter, L. W. and Lawler, E. E. (1968) 'Managerial attitudes and performance', cited in L. J. Mullins, *Management and Organisational Behaviour*, 1999, London: Pitman.

Psacharoupoulos, G. and Woodhall, M. (1985) *Education for Development*, Washington: World Bank.

Qualifications and Curriculum Authority (1998) *Education for citizenship and the teaching of democracy in schools, Part one: Advisory Group initial report*, London: QCA.

Radford, J. and Govier, E. (eds) (1991) *A Textbook of Psychology*, London: Routledge.

Raskin, P. M. (1994) 'Identity and the career counselling of adolescents: the development of vocational identity', in S. Archer (ed.) *Interventions for Adolescent Identity Development*, London: Sage.

Reddy, M. J. (1979) 'The conduit metaphor: a case of frame conflict in our language about language', in A. Ortony (ed.) *Metaphor and Thought*, Cambridge: Cambridge University Press.

Reece, I. and Walker, S. (1997) *Teaching and Learning*, Sunderland: Business Education.

Rodenburg, P. (1992) *The Right to Speak*, London: Methuen.

Rogers, C. (1961) *On Becoming A Person*, Boston: Houghton Mifflin.

——(1969) *Freedom to Learn: A View of What Education Might Become*, Columbus, Oh.: Charles E. Merrill.

——(1983) *Freedom to Learn for the 80's*, Columbus, Oh.: Charles E. Merrill.

Rorty, R. (1999) *Philosophy and Social Hope*, London: Penguin.

Rutter, M., Maugham, B., Mortimore, P. and Ouston, J. (1979) *Fifteen Thousand Hours: Secondary Schools and Their Effect on Children*, London: Open Books.

Säljö, R. (1979) Learning in the learner's perspective: I. Some common-sense conceptions, Reports from the Institute of Education, University of Gothenberg, 76, summarized in P. Banyard and N. Hayes (1994) *Psychology: Theory and Application*, London: Chapman & Hall.

Salmon, P. (1988) *Psychology for Teachers: an Alternative Approach*, London: Century Hutchison.

——(1995) *Psychology in the Classroom – Reconstructing Teachers and Learners*, London: Cassell.

Schön, D. (1983) *The Reflective Practitioner: How Professionals Think in Action*, New York: Basic Books.

Schön, D. (1987) *Educating the Reflective Practitioner*, San Francisco: Jossey-Bass.

Sharp, C. (1996) *Completion of A-level and GNVQ Courses in Schools*, Slough: NFER.

Sharp, P. (1998) 'The beginnings of GNVQs: an analysis of key determining events and factors', *Journal of Education and Work* 11: 3.

Silcock, P. (1993) 'Can we teach effective teaching?', *Educational Review* 45(1): 13–19.

Silver, H. (1999) *Researching Education: Themes in Teaching and Learning*, Bristol: The Policy Press.

Silver, R. (1995) 'Learning from 14', Lecture to the Royal Society of Arts, 15 March 1995, London: RSA Journal, July 1995: 70–79.

Smith, J. (2000) 'Schools minister finds out what young people want', London: DfEE, http://www.dfee.gov.uk/news.

Stenhouse, L. (1971) *Culture and Education*, London: Nelson.

—(ed.) (1980) *Curriculum Research and Development in Action*, London: Heinemann.

Stubbs, M. (1976) *Language, Schools and Classrooms*, London: Methuen.

Swann, J. (1992) *Girls, Boys and Language*, Oxford: Blackwell.

Taba, H. (1966) *Teaching Strategies and Cognitive Functioning in Elementary Schools*, Research Project 2004, Washington, DC: US Office of Education.

—(1967) *Teacher's Handbook to Elementary Social Studies*, Reading, MA: Addison-Wesley.

Tabberer, R. (1994) *School and Teacher Effectiveness*, Slough: National Foundation for Educational Research.

Taylor, R. (2000) 'Internet know-how', *Guardian Education*, p. 63.

Trades Union Congress (1989) *Skills 2000*, London: TUC.

Vroom, V. (1964) *Work and Motivation*, New York: Wiley, cited in G. Moorhead and R. W. Griffin (1992) *Organizational Behavior*, Boston: Houghton Mifflin Company.

Vygotsky, L. S. (1962) *Thought and Language*, Cambridge, MA: MIT Press.

—(1978) *Mind in Society*, Cambridge, MA: Harvard University Press.

Walker, J. (1995) *The Cost of Communication Breakdown*, Newcastle upon Tyne: Relate Centre for Family Studies.

Weston, P., Christophers, U., Schagen, I. and Lines, A. (1996) *Core Skills at Work*, Slough: NFER.

Wicks, M. (1999) 'Moving into the century of lifelong learning', interview with Brenda Kirsch of NATFHE, *The Lecturer*, December: 3.

Wilde, F. and Hardaker, R. (1997) 'Clarity is power: learning outcomes, learner autonomy and transferable skills', FEDA Report, 1, 10.

Wolf, A. (1995) *Competence-based Assessment*, Milton Keynes: Open University Press.

Wood, D., Bruner J. S. and Ross, G. (1976) 'The role of tutoring in problem solving', *Journal of Child Psychology and Psychiatry* 17: 89–100.

Wubbels, T. and Levy, J. (eds) (1993) *Do You Know What You Look Like? Interpersonal Relationships in Education*, London: Falmer.

Young, M. (1999) 'Reconstructing qualifications for further education: towards a system for the twenty-first century', in A. Green and N. Lucas (eds) *Further Education and Lifelong Learning: Realigning the Sector for the Twenty-first Century*, London: University of London Institute of Education.

Young, M., Lucas, N., Sharp, G. and Cunningham, B. (1995) *Teacher Education for the Further Education Sector: Training the Lecturer of the Future*, London: AFC/Institute of Education.

Young, R. (1992) *Critical Theory and Classroom Talk*, Clevedon: Multilingual Matters.

Index